WHITTAKER CHAMBERS

The Spirit of a Counterrevolutionary

Richard M. Reinsch II

ISI Books
Wilmington, Delaware

The Library of Modern Thinkers is published in cooperation with Collegiate Network, Inc. Generous grants from the Sarah Scaife Foundation, Earhart Foundation, F. M. Kirby Foundation, Castle Rock Foundation, Pierre F. and Enid Goodrich Foundation, Wilbur Foundation, and the William H. Donner Foundation made this series possible. The Intercollegiate Studies Institute and Collegiate Network, Inc., gratefully acknowledge their support.

Reinsch II, Richard M.

    Whittaker Chambers : the spirit of a counterrevolutionary / by Richard Reinsch.
    p. cm.—(Library of modern thinkers)
    Includes bibliographical references and index.
    ISBN 978-1-935191-52-0

    1. Chambers, Whittaker. 2. Spies—United States—Biography. 3. Journalists—United States—Biography. 4. Communism—United States—History—20th century I. Title.
E743.5.R45 2010
327.12092—dc22
[B]   2010013878

Published in the United States by:
ISI Books
3901 Centerville Road
Wilmington, DE 19807-1938
www.isibooks.org
Cover and interior design by Sam Torode

CONTENTS

Preface

WHILE RESEARCHING TOTALITARIANISM FOR AN academic conference, I encountered many impressive voices that analyzed Communist ideology and its noxious effects in the twentieth century.
But of all the voices, it was the odd-sounding one of Whittaker
Chambers that most illuminated this dark scene. The thought of
writing a book exploring his intellectual contributions struck me
as an act of recovery, one that would weave together the strands
of an enduring Chambers for future reflection. Years earlier, when
I read him as an undergraduate, Chambers had cast a devastating glance on the strange and jealous gods of the modern West
and their manifestation in the United States. However, the light
Chambers shone on his contemporary disorder—a light I had
received in my first pass through Chambers's epic autobiography,
Witness—remained inchoate, a brooding presence in my own
intellectual development.

Chambers's writings seemed also to me displaced. In the America of the last days of the twentieth century—dominant militarily, financially, and commercially, and the victor of the Cold War—his dire pronouncements seemed out of step with reality. Moreover, the conservative movement that Chambers had indelibly shaped was in its second return to prominence by way of the 1994 congressional elections at the same time I was reading *Witness*. The appeals made by conservative congressional hopefuls to the electorate largely consisted of arguments for material abundance or increasing the scope of individual choice. Such options would open to the citizen and consumer through welfare state retrenchment and the concomitant increase in purchasing power through market expansion. Nothing was more distant to the mournful spirit of Chambers's writings and witness against the hydra beast of totalitarianism and its anti-theist humanism and materialism. The conclusion seemed bare. The heaviness of Chambers's writing, accepted by the nascent conservative movement of his day, no longer seemed to contain insights that should be heeded by the statesman or the intellectual.

But what, in fact, should be said by a conservatism faced with such prosperity, or now, perhaps, decline? For this, one must return to the achievement of Whittaker Chambers, and the infusion of his spirit to what had become a nearly inanimate body of thought, smoldering underground, while the aims of the New Deal were being concretized in the nation's experience. This fact, coupled with the near-constant advancement of Communist ideology, spoke to Chambers of the need for recovery halfway into the twentieth century.

To be sure, this quest, when conducted under a different intellectual dispensation, had originally led Chambers to Communism, for which he served first as a journalist, writer, and essayist, and then as an underground courier and contact. In his initial attempt to resolve the apparently broken condition of the modern West Chambers discovered that salvation by technique, in this case, perfection through Communist government, was illusory and murderous. This insight, which eluded many of his contemporaries, uncovered a much larger idea—man's problem was the problem of understanding himself in light of his fundamental incompleteness.

Communism was the most logical extension and application of several ideas that had held sway over modernity since the Continental Enlightenment, Chambers believed. These had all pointed to man's singular capacity to order the political, social, and economic realms by finally resolving through univocal reason the sufferings and mistakes that had dogged man throughout his existence. Reason's enthronement had promised a type of liberation. Against this intellectual backdrop of a human existence conceived as limitless possibility Chambers came to affirm precisely the opposite. If everything was possible to modern man, according to the new intellectual priesthood, Chambers sounded that man was never more beastly than in his attempts to organize his life, individually and collectively, without God.

Chambers's largest political act was his testimony in front of the House Committee on Un-American Activities in 1948 against Alger Hiss for acts of treason Hiss committed while a high-ranking official at the United States Department of State. Following on Hiss's indictment by a federal grand jury was a series of dramatic events that led to his later conviction for perjury in 1950. Chambers's testimony against Hiss, as he instructed in *Witness,* was to punish past and forestall current and future treason by government officials with direct and indirect ties to the Soviet government. The case's larger meaning—for its factual narrative rests beyond impeachment—is betrayal of both nation and the very spirit of man through allegiance to an ideology which recognizes neither.

In describing Chambers I have continually held two pictures of him in my mind, twinned aspects of the existence he lived as a Communist and, then, as a free man. One depiction is of Chambers ambling down the streets of Washington, DC, pilfered documents in tow, serving the Soviet Union in the most conspiring of ways, having betrayed his country in the process. The picture contains not only a Communist Chambers, but a compartmentalized man, loving family on one day and, on another, hauling stolen federal government documents to clandestine locations, as an underground courier. It is an incomplete Chambers, much like the revolution he sought to serve—a life that succeeds only by the gross subjugation of greater truths. As Communism denied man his full being, so Chambers, as an underground agent, existed through transgression of country and his spirit.

The other scene is Chambers, this time his hands joined to the soil and to the care of his cattle and sheep at his farm in ancient Maryland, engaged in what British commentator Rebecca West termed Chambers's "Christian Pantheism." West's observation certainly accords with the inspiration and repose Chambers drew from agricultural labor. In his last decade, Chambers's laborious tasks of writing and farming proved sanctifying. A life seemingly wrecked by the storms that crushed millions of men found its meaning—the measure of reality—in the life of a yeoman farmer. From this labor came a strange hope, albeit a fleeting one, and from it came *Witness* and the later collections of writings left for posterity: writings that contain a life that gave the eloquence of truth to an age and people unwilling to embrace it.

In reading Chambers one does well to remember his final teaching in the last paragraph of "Letter to My Children." His son's and daughter's hands, Chambers informs them, will slip from his grasp; however, "It will not matter." Their father will have shown them the path to tread; they are now ready to see and walk alone. Separate paths will not mean separate destinations or disparate meanings. "For when you understand what you see, you will no longer be children. You will know that life is pain, that each of us hangs always upon the cross of himself. And when you know that this is true of every man, woman and child on earth, you will be wise."

Richard M. Reinsch II
Beaufort, SC
December 2008

CHAPTER ONE

THE PROJECT OF A COUNTERREVOLUTIONARY

There in the desert I lay dead, And God called out to me and said: "Rise, prophet, rise, and hear, and see, And let my works be seen and heard by all who turn aside from me, And burn them with my fiery word."

—Alexander Pushkin, *The Prophet*[1]

UPON FIRST GLANCE ONE MAY inquire why the contemporary world needs a book on the thought of Whittaker Chambers. After all, the focus of Chambers's anti-Communist witness and writings, which was the seeming inability of a complacent United States to stop the ideologically confident Soviet Union in its internationalist machinations, has passed. For Chambers, this weakness was never more prominently revealed than in America's difficulties in confronting and condemning the unrepentant Communist traitor in its midst, Alger Hiss. The Hiss–Chambers case is now with certain exceptions infrequently remarked upon from any significant corner of American political thought.[2] One of the central events of twentieth century American political life, signifying the existence of multiple social and political conflicts within the nation, the impact of the Hiss–Chambers case has also passed with time.

The indifference or hostility with which Chambers is held, even by members of the conservative movement he helped shape, has also been detrimental to Chambers's legacy. In many ways, Chambers's current reputation seems to be colored by the dominant narrative that emerged from Communism's end. The extinction of Communism as a viable project and the dilapidated state of the societies and nations that kneeled under its weight taught integral lessons, material and spiritual, on the conditions for human flourishing in modernity. The post-Cold War Western consensus has seemed to resist the full weight of these lessons. By viewing the failure of Communism as an inevitable conclusion because the ideology was on the wrong side of history, the Western consensus has paradoxically held to an essentially Marxist understanding of history. In this analysis, the West could not fail in its confrontation with Communist forces. Chambers's sacrifices in abandoning Communism and testifying against Alger Hiss become superfluous under this historical narrative.

Another significant trend that surfaced after Communism's collapse was the trumpeting to Russia and its former satellite nations, rightfully so in certain respects, the values of individualism, free markets, promarket tax policies, and democratically elected governments. The central lesson learned by the West (including many in the American conservative movement) from Communism's implosion was the unparalleled and exclusive ability of free markets and other democratic institutions to deliver material benefits and goods to members of a free society. Consequently, the belief in the mind of man and its ability to achieve a rational political, economic, and social order, while relatively unconcerned with transcendent loyalties, was and remains in place.

Chambers would not have been surprised by this "official version" that his nation or the West would tell itself about Communism's demise. The official version's incipient materialism renders Chambers's act of witness and self-sacrifice largely one of antiquated interest. The man who saw the Cold War as a contest between two great faiths—Communism or Freedom, God or Man—is now singularly reduced to an informant. If Chambers's significance concerns only the testimony that committed Alger Hiss to prison and alerted a nation to certain Communists and fellow travelers in government posts, then he has rendered his service in full to our country. We can adulate him, insofar as his efforts moved us closer to victory over Communism by spotlighting its internal clandestine efforts, and then forget him. The Cold War is over, and impersonal materialist forces earned us the victory.[3]

The apparent meanings of history, however, often hide realities that remain in flux. The Western policy illuminati that initially flooded into post-Soviet Russia treated the political and economic regeneration of the country in largely technocratic terms. The rule of law, democratic institutions, and a relatively free market were capable of being built and sustained with no formal commitment to civil society and local self-government, orthodox religion, the family, morality, or the human spirit.[4] The continuing obstacles to a stable system of ordered liberty in Russia, and in many of its former socialist fiefdoms, attest to the Cold War being more than a Manichean standoff on the most efficient methods of market organization. In its current struggle to create and, at times, failure to sustain the institutions necessary for liberty, Russia highlights the delicacy of free institutions and the convictions required of a citizenry to maintain them. It seems the deprivation of man's spirit, as Chambers recognized, produces wounds not easily healed by enlightened policy.

To understand the chasm between the official version of Communism's demise and Chambers's admonishments, one must look to the foundation of his anti-Communist witness. Chambers's witness was forged by his exit from the Soviet Underground apparatus in 1938 and his testimony before the House Committee on Un-American Activities in 1948.[5] His witness, however, was more than courtroom testimony, acts of irrepressible will, or the tactics of counterespionage which he so efficiently deployed in his run from underground Communist authorities.[6] The literary, theological, and philosophical Chambers is excluded when his acts of grace, daring, and will are given myopic focus. This equal, and perhaps more enduring, legacy makes an important contribution to a modern society seeking to balance the human requirement for liberty with moral authority.

Part of the record that is not considered in many analyses of Chambers are the ten years of journalism, short stories, and various other pieces he produced between 1938 and 1948 as an editor and later senior editor at *Time* magazine.[7] In this position, Chambers leveraged his massive talent and the Henry Luce media empire to reach tens of millions of American homes. The editorial posture he brought was a penetrating moral and spiritual clarity applied to a range of subjects, thinkers, and contemporaneous and historical events. Later, as senior editor of the foreign news desk, Chambers performed acts of intellectual repentance for his Communist past by articulating a determined antitotalitarian position, and by continually analyzing the works of twentieth century intellectuals who grappled with the modern mind's distance from God.[8]

Chambers's journalism draws the reader in under the intimation that it holds an abstruse passageway to truth amidst the previous century of chaos. Two essays in particular, "Silence, Exile, and Death" and "In Egypt Land," published in 1941 and 1946 respectively, develop ideas integral to Chambers's posttrial writing. These essays depict artists who never lost their connection, however tenuous it may have been, to the truth of beauty amidst pressing circumstances. However confused man becomes on the matter, truth (or in Chambers's term, reality) is the only thing that a man desires, especially near his end, and is the only thing he takes with him at his death.

Chambers's account of James Joyce's last months in "Silence, Exile, and Death" portrayed Joyce's gradual diminishment of hope during the Nazi onslaught of France in 1940. Caught between the grasps of totalitarian power and the bumbling efforts of liberal democracies, Joyce's predicament illustrated Chambers's view of the characteristic experience in the age of total crisis: the solitary individual interned and then broken by overwhelming forces.[9] After months of detainment in Vichy France, Joyce finally crossed into neutral Switzerland where his last comfort was not writing, but delivering to his young grandson's ear the words of his civilization's grand poets before it crumbled.[10]

"Silence, Exile, and Death" symbolized the errors of modern thought with its implication that Joyce was unable to find refuge within a liberal regime. The artist, the articulator of the beautiful, finds no haven within modernity's restrained political regime of liberal democracy; it is unable to repel, as it were, the vicious elements of the totalitarian state. Art itself, Chambers communicated, may no longer be possible under the weight of modern ideology as it expressed itself in both liberal democracy and the totalitarian state.

The essay "In Egypt Land," on the black contralto Marian Anderson, was a haunting piece about the human soul's incipient desire for beauty and truth.[11] The crushing experience of racial injustice suffered by black Americans was ominous in the essay's background. Anderson, the consummate musical artist, was an archetype of the tyrannized soul that reached beyond pain and strife, bypassing anger and grievance, to touch beauty itself. Chambers expressed the idea that Anderson's Christianity formed the measure of her resistance to injustice. Thus, political justice was approached through the beauty of faith and love, a soulful movement that Chambers would emulate in the years ahead.

While not a permanent feature of her concerts, the classically trained Anderson at times performed Negro Spirituals. In commenting on Anderson's public use of the spiritual, Chambers poignantly said:

> One simple fact is clear—they [the spirituals] were created in direct answer to the Psalmist's question: *How shall we sing the Lord's song in a strange land?* For the land in which the slaves found themselves was strange beyond the

fact that it was foreign. It was a nocturnal land of vast, shadowy pine woods, vast fields of cotton whose endless rows converged sometimes on a solitary cabin, vast swamps reptilian and furtive—a land alive with all the elements of lonely beauty, except compassion. In this deep night of land and man, the singers saw visions; grief, like a tuning fork, gave the tone, and the Sorrow Songs were uttered.[12]

The mode of Anderson's reach was divinity, guiding the artist toward a rarefied solemnity never more on display than during her renditions of the "Sorrow Songs," which reinforced Chambers's belief that intractable disorders in the city of man—like racial oppression and segregation—could only find peace through repentance, self-limitation, and other movements of the human spirit.[13] Although the intervention of law was necessary, the modernist desire for the pure political solution ignored man's essence as person. Chambers believed that Anderson, as artist and Christian, was emblematic of the graced approach to love and truth that the modern American must make to remedy America's original sin of racial subjugation.

Chambers's posttrial writing expanded many of the ideas he articulated in his journalism career, only now held against the belief that his individual efforts against Hiss and Communism were likely to end in failure. Chambers opened his autobiography, *Witness*—first published in 1952—with the straightforward assertion that in leaving Communism he was joining the "Losing Side."[14] This assertion shocked Americans in the 1950s and still appears absurd to most contemporary readers. To Chambers, however, there were no apparent signs on the West's horizon to convince him otherwise. Striking confirmation was provided, he believed, by the failure of America, and the West as a whole, to support the Hungarian Resistance in 1956.[15] Spurred by the de-Stalinization launched by Soviet leader Nikita S. Khrushchev in February of 1956, three years after Joseph Stalin's death, Hungarians revolted violently against their Communist government in October 1956. Having secured an initial victory, the Hungarian revolutionaries were crushed by Soviet troops, who stormed into Budapest on November 4, 1956, and retook the city.

A new meaning of reality in the Cold War had become possible because of the Resistance. The rejection of Communism in favor of Hungarian patriotism and a national political life liberated from Soviet exploitations was clearly evident. Such a reality, however, was not to be enacted. Chambers blamed American indecisiveness, which was distracted by the Suez Canal Crisis, among other crises of will, for its refusal to supply aid of any kind to the Hungarian patriots. Disconsolate at the failure of American will in the affair, Chambers quoted a Hungarian revolutionary to summarize his gloom: "you [Americans] did not even organize a gun-running service for us."[16]

Chambers's belief in the pervasiveness and perniciousness of philosophical materialism loomed large in his expectation of defeat. While such materialism had inspired and directed the project of Communism, Chambers held that it had also been assumed into the political and economic order of the Western nations.[17] Therefore, the West's weakness in the face of internationalist Communist aggression was a consequence of its affinity to the philosophical suppositions guiding the Communist juggernaut.

Chambers insisted that the West's only chance of victory was through suffering, in which the West might summon the will to survive by recovering its former spirits and surmounting its deadening materialism.[18] Chambers remained doubtful of this possibility throughout his life.

In *Cold Friday,* a collection of his essays and letters, posthumously published in 1964, Chambers discussed man's inherent need for belief and for worship, both individually as people, and collectively as a nation. Written at his relatively isolated Maryland farm, years after the Hiss Trial, *Cold Friday* also shows a man still mired in the trial and its aftermath. This is not surprising and yet it is not the whole picture.

In these essays, Chambers demonstrated poetic wonder at redemption and its accompanying inescapable logic of suffering. According to Chambers, the capability to endure suffering was a predicate to the thriving existence of any civilization. The avoidance of suffering and its "hourly and daily dying" led inevitably to an existence alienated from the deeper springs of love and honor that propel a culture and nation forward.[19] This certainty of the demise of civilization issued from the "incapacity for growth" and "infantilism" of a culture wedded to the avoidance of suffering.[20] In such a culture, nothing would be loved much or ventured much. Floating in the lukewarm pool of creature comforts, such an undeserving people would finally lose even those comforts.

Chambers's conception of true despair was that which kills both body and soul through foreclosing the free attempt to enact existential truth. In this way modern man became ahistorical: man ceased to see the purpose of his own being. Faith's evaporation left him rudderless in the modern age. Bursting from this complacency was the Communist, and though he destroys himself and others, his purpose was to act again with meaning.[21] Lurking in this formulation was the idea that Communism's cause and existence were tied to the loss of faith.

Recalling saintly wisdom, Chambers counseled that suffering and tragedy are not authentic sources of despair; rather, they are inherent to man's need to find the measure of his meaning in the brief time allotted to him.[22] The price of suffering is real but its crown is liberation. The man formed under its tutelage knows his true end and the authentic freedom it offers. Such beauty cannot be had for any lower price.[23]

Perhaps the best way to understand *Cold Friday* is to read the book's self-titled essay in which Chambers outlined why he removed his family to a farm in rural Maryland. Chambers always had a soulful longing for place, community, and joyful labor.[24] Further, Cold Friday, Chambers's beloved field at his Westminster farm, afforded him "Height," and the opportunity to understand and to reflect upon the forces that broke against him. Impossible to cultivate because of its elevation, the fallow field prepared the way for thought, as well as faith and hope. From Cold Friday, the understanding of truth was now possible, but not without wearisome toil. As Chambers said, "We must reach [truth] by crawling on our hands and knees."[25] Upon reaching Cold Friday the view was "not what we might . . . pray for, but what really is . . . [and then we find our meaning] in our own reality."[26] Chambers's reality was the outcome of perception and the consequent measuring of the forces around him by reflection and prayer. The experience

Chambers described required a high level of honesty and love for the attempt to be made. This cognitive and spiritual veracity kept the struggle from being mere solipsism. At Cold Friday, man wrestled with his incompleteness before the infinite in order to know realities definite and enduring.[27]

The farm and the field were in turn places of defense for Chambers and his family from the crushing weight of modernity. This notion was epitomized in Chambers's fascination with the opening line from Aeschylus's *Prometheus Bound,* wherein Power says to Force and Prometheus: "We have come to the last path of the world, in the Scythian country, in the untrodden solitude."[28] Modern man's Promethean attempts to overcome his mortal incompleteness by a mindless exaltation of political and economic revolution had proven illusory and horrific. The ostensible satiety found in this quest was devastating. Spurred by his commitment to the Communist vision, Chambers had crawled over several fields only to realize the abyss that had enveloped him. Cold Friday thus stood for the end of Chambers's own Promethean striving. Chambers declared on this score:

> Here I determined to root the lives of my children—to live here and die here in this particular earth. On this earth, I was determined, our line would remain or end. Thus, for me, Cold Friday stands also for all the fields a man must cross to reach it.[29]

Chambers's other purpose at Cold Friday was to root his family in the land and manfully build upon tradition. Chambers said:

I was also fully conscious of another resolve: to end the
wanderings of my house which for generations has been
in flight westward—Huguenot fugitives from France to
Ireland, as soldiers from Holland to Britain, as revolutionists fleeing from Ireland and Scotland to America.[30]

Chambers's family lineage was fully American in its searching and
travelling. By conjoining with modern ideology in Chambers's
effort at secular certainty, this familial striving had taken on an
entirely new form. His search was not geographical or vocational
but rather an existential quest for meaning in a crazed world.
However, the grace of old truths freshly rediscovered had united
Chambers to the land. The farm was to be Chambers's final home
and the only lasting, tangible reality he could give his children.[31]
Chambers's correspondence with William F. Buckley Jr. shared
many of *Cold Friday's* themes, but it also revealed something more
of Chambers.[32] Hope, as a virtue, seemed to elude Chambers, pre-
venting him from finally resting and enjoying the habit of being.
One senses in these letters that Chambers was embattled on two
fronts. His larger struggle with Communism was conducted simultaneously with other struggles elemental to his personal existence.
Doubt and weariness hovered around him in much of the Buckley
correspondence. There was a brief period during the Hiss trial
when Chambers even attempted suicide, but whatever physical or
psychological pain that enveloped Chambers, he strove forward
both for his family and for the "children of men."

In the Buckley correspondence Chambers frequently demonstrated certainty of the projects and ends that must be achieved

by the nascent Right in America, and yet, strangely, he was quite moderate in his tactical advice.[33] Aware of his ends, Chambers indicated a willingness to employ a variety of means and tactics in political action. He was, however, reluctant to fully embrace Buckley's (and *National Review*'s) conservative individualism. The emerging strength of the fusionism articulated by *National Review* editor Frank S. Meyer, while not distasteful to Chambers, never filled him with inspiration for the conservative position in America. A former man of the Left and a postwar, intellectual conservative, Frank Meyer sought to bridge the libertarian and conservative divide, with his notion of maximum individual freedom to permit the meaningful opportunity of virtuous action. Chambers, however, thought this idea overlooked the nature of politics in modern representative government. Rather, Chambers's political strategy required a Republican Left and, perhaps, a Religious Left—an assemblage of Americans of steady patriotism and religious faith who held to a profound love for American cultural norms, which excused their patchy commitment to capitalism and small government—to add heft to American conservatism in order for a measurable blow to be struck against political revolution.[34]

Moreover, Chambers believed that counterrevolutionary politics meant never losing sight of the enemy's ability to distort your ideological stridency into their psychological rallying cry. Chambers believed *National Review*'s (and much of the American Right's) embrace of Senator Joseph McCarthy was an unforced error. However effective the Wisconsin senator may initially have been, Chambers felt McCarthy lacked judgment and believed that through abuse certain victories were possible. On McCarthy's technique, Chambers opined, "[I]t is repetitious and unartful, and, with time, the repeated dull thud of the low blow may prove to be the real factor in his undoing."[35] Senator McCarthy's incoherent strategy and general imprudence led Chambers to refuse an alliance with him. Chambers made his position clear in his advice to Buckley to refrain from coupling conservatism with the Wisconsin senator.[36] In Chambers's estimation, McCarthy had become the fusionist manqué for Communist forces who, unable to maneuver in America, depended on a popular front strategy for their advances. Ultimately, Chambers believed himself the repository of trust in the anti-Communist fight. Such trust had to be husbanded with great care lest it be depleted or fretted on those men who divided the Right and united the Left as McCarthy had done.[37]

The Ralph de Toledano correspondence, entitled *Notes from the Underground,* shows Chambers as a man for whom thought and act must be equally heroic in the age of modern revolution.[38] Toledano covered the Hiss case for *Newsweek.* Having interviewed Chambers before the actual trial, the two men had come to admire one another and formed an abiding friendship. Toledano later co-authored a book with Victor Lasky called *Seeds of Treason*—published in 1950—that gave an unparalleled account of the Hiss case by its documentation of the relationships and influence of Hiss and other Communists inside the federal government. The book, unlike many others on the Hiss case, was quite favorable to Chambers's claims regarding Hiss's guilt.

Chambers's true light in the Toledano correspondence was found in a series of letters in which he sharply attacked the efforts of playwright Sol Stein to dramatize the Hiss trial. Stein's stage production focused heavily on the trial's political intrigue to the detriment of the existential commitments made by Chambers and Hiss. Chambers's version of events eluded Stein who was inept at understanding the unfolding of forces that happened at the Hiss trial. The enduring imprint of the trial, so monumental in Chambers's conception, remained hidden from many cultural commentators of the period, including Stein.[39] Stein's play entitled *A Shadow of My Enemy* ran for a week at the American National Theatre and Academy in New York, and garnered less than enthusiastic reviews.[40] Chambers wrote that the play was hopelessly misconceived by the director and needed to be rejected by all concerned with the full import of the Hiss trial.[41]

Because Stein lacked a proper understanding of Chambers and Hiss, the trial's true significance evaded Stein at every turn. The artistic production was a hopeless caricature in Chambers's mind: these men were revolutionaries, not marionettes. Neither Chambers nor Hiss sought personal glory or power; rather, both men were willing to immolate themselves to advance their guard, "to make that quantum leap of humanity and history possible."[42] As Chambers reasoned, "The Hiss case, including *Witness,* was the effort of a man to hurl himself against the rationalism which must destroy the world, and seems to be on the point of doing so. It was a lunge against Communism *chiefly as the logical, the inevitable epitome of that rationalism.*"[43] Exasperated with Stein, Chambers wrote to Toledano, "Tell Stein to keep away from the artillery fire. He does not know what type of war this is."[44]

More important than the production norms of the Communist or the low prices and profit margins of the capitalist, Chambers and

Hiss were forces for exalted meaning and purpose.[45] Regarding their actions, Chambers observed, "In terms of realism, neither Alger nor I can exist, because, in terms of the real world (Communism with capitalist deformations, or capitalism with socialist deformations), people do not die for their beliefs. People clip coupons, or try to apply the general line correctly, or pass production norms. Hiss and I are asserting something beyond reality. . . ."[46] This was the tragedy of their encounter: both men believed and were prepared to go to the end for their truths. Stein, in his unbelief, never grasped this notion, and so he was left shrouding Hiss and Chambers in "realistic ritual." Chambers provided, perhaps, a fitting summation when he said, "And do you think that real communists, in the secrecy of the lodge, do not know my inches?" Chambers never slipped in his intellectual and corresponding volitional commitments.

The power of Chambers's political commitments was never more evident than in his account of his break with Communism. The first page of *Witness* informs the reader of the depths from which Chambers returned when he left the service of the Communist Party and the underground apparatus of the Fourth Section of Soviet Military Intelligence.[47] Chambers opened with the following line, "In 1937, I began, like Lazarus, the impossible return. I began to break away from Communism and to climb from deep within its underground, where for six years I had been buried, back into the world of free men."[48] Continuing the theme of a Lazarus-like rebirth Chambers quoted Henrik Ibsen in the same passage: "When we dead awaken. . . ."[49] If Chambers through grace, both common and divine, had decided to return to the world of free men why, then, did he leave it in the first instance?

The Middle Class and the Total Crisis

According to Chambers, the story of his descent into the inferno of modernist ideology began in a former postal coach stop that was the Chambers's family home in Lynbrook, New York, situated at the edge of then undeveloped Long Island. Whittaker Chambers was born Jay Vivian Chambers on April 1, 1901, in Philadelphia. The Chambers family did not move to Lynbrook until approximately three years after the birth of Whittaker's younger brother Richard in 1903. Chambers's father Jay was a graphic artist for the *New York World* and later a designer of book covers and magazine illustrations having lost his *World* job to "technological unemployment."[50] In Lynbrook, Chambers began to show the serious and severe traits of character that marked him throughout his life.

Rejected by a father who never loved his two sons or his wife, Chambers affably described the peace he found in the wooded areas and shoreline near his home.[51] In *Witness,* Chambers related his childhood experience:

> I stood up, on the other side, in a field covered from end to end, as high as my head, with thistles in full bloom. Clinging to the purple flowers, hovering over them, or twittering and dipping in flight, were dozens of goldfinches—little golden yellow birds with black, contrasting wings and caps. They did not pay the slightest attention to me, as if they had never seen a boy before.
>
> The sight was so unexpected, the beauty was so abso-

lute, that I thought I could not stand it and held to the hedge for support. Out loud, I said: "God." It was a simple statement, not an exclamation, of which I would then have been incapable. At that moment, which I remembered through all the years of my life as one of the highest moments, I was closer than I would be again for almost forty years to the intuition that alone could give meaning to my life—the intuition that God and beauty are one.[52]

The tranquility of coastal Lynbrook provided haven in the early morning hours for the adolescent Chambers to stalk its shores before other family members had risen. The same man who would later speak sonorously of Cold Friday found this tune early in life in response to similar needs for space amid the weight of crushing forces.[53]

Such peace was a necessity in Chambers's life at Lynbrook. He was rejected by his father early and often, principally exhibited by Jay's departure from the family when Chambers was only seven. Although Jay returned two years later, he lived in the home more as a boarder than as head of the household. He took his meals in private, rarely emerging from his retreat within their home.[54] Laha Whittaker, Chambers's mother, also lived with the pain of Jay's rejection and turned this loss into a doting, almost smothering, love for Whittaker and Richard.

Laha's pain also stemmed from other aspects of the burgeoning modern America. Laha's father had made and lost more than one fortune, and the dream she held of collegiate life in the east went unmet due to his last reversal of fortune. The family finally moved from Chicago to New York City where they lived a hardscrabble existence running a diner. Laha's short period as a travelling thespian was now over, and her father—who died from cancer at age fifty-nine—had left the family penniless with only an insufficient Civil War soldier's pension. At thirty, Laha married Jay Chambers, a frequent customer at the family eatery which was located near the offices of the *New York World*. In some ways a social elevation, their marriage was never able to slake Laha's urgency for respectability, status, and upper-middle class wealth. One might surmise that Chambers's lifelong distaste for commercial behavior emerged at the Lynbrook home of a lady and mother never satisfied, always yearning for the standard of the bourgeois capitalist.

The failure of his middle-class family fueled many of Chambers's later decisions and commitments. While a student at Columbia University, Chambers came to see the world in perpetual failure and brokenness, but this worldview originally sprang from his family life in Lynbrook. Never fully embraced by their father and left with a harrowed mother, Chambers and his brother shared the conviction that their family's brokenness was symptomatic and causally linked to a larger existential crisis in their society.[55] Triggered by this initial gloom of a broken family, Chambers looked towards the Marxist solution to this societal crisis.

The beneficiary of a new admissions policy that ushered in students from across New York State upon satisfactory completion of an "intelligence test," Chambers entered Columbia University in the fall of 1920.[56] A self-styled Republican, adamant supporter of Calvin Coolidge, and a Christian Scientist, Chambers for the first time displayed, and was recognized for, his uncommon intellectual abilities.[57] The high intensity of Chambers's political commitments first surfaced at Columbia. During his freshman year Chambers led a solo campaign for Coolidge's 1920 election run by dispatching pro-Coolidge letters to newspapers across America. At one point, the freshman scaled a fire escape to catch a glimpse of Coolidge at a campaign appearance.[58]

At Columbia, Chambers merged his creeping intellectual austerity and literary endowment with his propensity for writing short stories and plays for campus publications. His first short story "The Damn Fool" was published in *The Morningside,* an undergraduate literary periodical, and featured the actions of a pseudo-Christian martyr killed while leading a contingent of White Army soldiers in a hopeless fight against Bolshevik forces. The piece earned Chambers praise and rarefied notice amongst the literary community of Columbia. The greater significance of the story was the projection of the main character's humility through sacrifice leading to martyrdom.[59] The connection between the actions of the play's protagonist and Chambers's much later decision to inform against Hiss and others in the federal government is quite telling. The story was more than Chambers's literary imagination; in constructing "The Damn Fool" Chambers also revealed his moral-philosophical ideal.

Other pieces followed, but "A Play for Puppets," an ill-advised attempt at daring authenticity, replete with atheist derision of Christian doctrines, merited censure from administrators, and Chambers removed himself from school. This exit was a pivotal turn for Chambers's intellectual development. Possessed of newfound liberty, Chambers travelled in 1923 to a Europe still recovering from World War I. In Germany and France Chambers initially encountered what he termed in *Witness* "the total crisis."[60]

Germany and France, two nations that were central to the Western tradition, had been rendered feeble and impotent by the new industrialized warfare of the modern democracies. On a train ride through France Chambers observed the bare remains of entire villages and towns destroyed by the shelling during the Great War. Chambers further saw that Germany, reeling under extreme inflation and large-scale social turmoil, was broken and disheveled as well. Chambers described one of his experiences in Germany:

> Well-dressed people walked back and forth along the Kurfürstendamm, like any Fifth Avenue crowd. Suddenly, the tears would stream down a woman's face simply as she walked along—the face of desperation, which asked and expected neither pity nor help, for there was not pity or help because there was no hope. The commonest of sights was to see someone snatch a purse and disappear in the crowd which rushed together for a moment, attracted by the victim's cries, and then walked on again with a shrug.[61]

Although Germany seemed to suffer the same fate as the other European powers, another breed of human opened to Chambers there whom he depicted as "little knots of furtive figures selling newspapers at some of the street corners . . . They were selling *Die Rote Fahne* [*The Red Flag*, a Communist newspaper]."[62] In a land of uncertainty and desperation, it was the Communists, repressed by authority, who were quite sure of their purpose and solution. The point was not lost on twenty-three-year-old Chambers.

Chambers's crisis of faith during his European adventure was by no means a first impression. Initially prompted by his family's failings, doubt had crept in and begun to root in Chambers at Columbia. Under the influence of a fashionable skepticism as a student, Chambers largely shed his religious beliefs and political conservatism. The instructor Mark van Doren played a lead role in deconstructing what Chambers termed his "crude" beliefs. The young Chambers reported his intense admiration for van Doren as an intellectual and became susceptible both to van Doren's Leftism and religious skepticism. In different conversations with his professor, Chambers noted that he came away believing that his "intellectual shirttails were showing," and thinking that "my religious gropings were not a little childish."[63]

Chambers biographer Sam Tanenhaus commented, "Chambers was less a blasphemer than a tormented doubter, hungry for a sustaining faith."[64] Chambers stated that it was "liberalism" that was to "perform on me its historic task in our times."[65] His "immature and patchwork beliefs" were dismantled at a steady pace. Chambers recalled that his "sense that some things are true and some things are false was to yield to the moral relativity summed up by Hamlet and quoted by one of my instructors: 'There is nothing good or bad but thinking makes it so.'"[66] Chambers related that his mind soon became a "hodgepodge" leaving behind belief in a "crude conservative order."[67] The characteristic task of liberalism now accomplished, Chambers believed, briefly, in nothing. The despair that Chambers developed at Columbia soon gave way to belief in substantive ideological forces at work in "the crisis of history in the twentieth century."[68]

The final event that occurred on Chambers's narrow path to Communist fervor was Richard Chambers's suicide on September 8, 1926. Chambers's verse reveals his own state:

My brother lies in the cold earth,
A cold rain is overhead.
My brother lies in the cold earth,
A sheet of ice is over his head.
The cold earth holds him round;
A sheet of ice is over his face.
My brother has no more
The cold rain to face.[69]

Chambers recorded in *Witness:* "Life that could destroy so gentle a nature as my brother's was meaningless."[70] Or so it seemed in the immediate aftermath of Richard's death. Ideas, events, and persons had not congealed for some time in Chambers's orbit, but unlike Richard, he had found resolve in the dark night. Chambers emerged from his despair with an objective: Communism. One night after visiting his brother's grave Chambers committed to be a thorough-going Communist. While Chambers was a Communist prior to Richard's suicide—he was a Party member by 1925—his devotion to the revolutionary cause intensified after his brother's death.[71] Chambers's newfound resolve notwithstanding, he lamented that this meant he could not join his brother.[72]

The form and matter of Chambers's particularized service to

Communism were not long hidden. The future underground agent, perplexed by the maniacal behavior of many fellow party members, found his spiritual center not in the minutiae of dialectical theorizing, but in those Communists who embodied its historical calling. The example of a Hungarian Communist patron of the New York Public Library where Chambers worked confirmed his belief. Intellectually, the patron imparted little, as most of the insights he relayed to Chambers were available in Lenin's classic text *What is to be Done*.[73] The aestheticism of the Hungarian's Communism was what most impressed Chambers and what led him to remark that he was "the most thoroughly integrated human being I had ever met, and the one most responsible for turning me into a real Bolshevik."[74] In a later reflection, Chambers compared the Hungarian Communist's living quarters to a monk's room of the twentieth century, that is, "a Communist's room."[75]

The Soul's Emancipation from Ideology

The philosophical and theological underpinnings of his formal break with Communism and underground activities in 1938 were pivotal to Chambers's antitotalitarian witness. The facts of Chambers's life within, and his exit from, the Communist Party and underground apparatus are well documented. The task at hand, however, is to understand the connecting ideational threads that led Chambers into and out of Communism and to atone for his and the West's tragic vision in the twentieth century.

As a Communist, Chambers married Esther Shemitz, first noticing her when she led a counter charge of striking workers into the teeth of police forces. Esther, who largely shared in Chambers's Communism, bore him two children prior to his decision to abandon the Soviet Underground cell he was leading.[76] Whittaker and Esther's children, Ellen and John, were their principal concern as the family hid and skirted existence in the fateful days of 1938 until Chambers found employment as the books editor at *Time.* Equipped with the same resolve as her husband, Esther's detailed testimony during the Hiss trial added further evidence of the profound connection between the Chamberses and the Hisses. At trial, Esther recalled the various Hiss domiciles with frightening accuracy. Her memory proved vital when she testified to the shape and contents of the last Hiss home. The defense claimed that she had never seen it.[77] She also held their family together during the dislocations they experienced after Whittaker's defection from the Soviet Underground. Money was so scarce during this period that Whittaker and Esther regularly skipped meals, begged from friends, and haggled with pawnbrokers.[78] Esther remained devoted to Chambers through all of these harrowing experiences. When Hiss's counsel, Lloyd Stryker, implied to Esther during her testimony that her husband was not decent and honorable, she replied, almost spontaneously, "I resent that! My husband is a decent citizen, a great man!"[79] Many persons and circumstances failed Chambers, his wife never did.

In "Letter to my Children," Chambers detailed two movements of the soul that pushed him from the Communist lair. The first movement was hearing screams coming from Communism's victims. Terror, in Chambers's formulation, was an unavoidable partner for the Communist in the execution of his vision. The logic was both brutal and simple. According to the Marxist–Leninist point of view, the laws of history were capable of providing the perfection necessary for man's final elevation from his near-constant suffering at the hands of injustice. Death and imprisonment logically followed for those standing athwart the dialectical process and its consummation in universal peace.[80] Terror, as a handmaid, superimposed the Communist vision onto the limitless suffering plaguing mankind. The screams evoked the basic struggles that raged in men who denied the soul in the same instant that they experienced horror at the hands of their own ideology.[81]

The power of the screams nullified the inexorable logic of materialist Communism by isolating the party member with the unwelcome knowledge of the morbid price paid by Communist victims. Such communication was unpreventable by the Communist Party and was the inevitable outcome of terror as legitimate policy. The screams pierced beyond the level of mind, history, and politics and reached to the soul, vindicating the essence of the person. Chambers described their effect:

> Those are not the screams of a man in agony. Those are the screams of a soul in agony. He hears them for the first time because a soul in extremity has communicated with that which alone can hear it—another human soul.[82]

Exhausted by these inexplicable phenomena, reason and logic explain very little, if anything, in the presence of the screams. If the party member listens attentively, then he acknowledges his conscience and its humble stance before divinity: "He has brushed the only vision that has force against . . . Almighty Mind. He stands before the fact of God."[83] The screams commune with the soul and are a signpost to God. For Chambers, God was always the prime mover in the war between Communism and freedom. If God exists then Communism cannot.

The second movement occurred when Chambers noticed the intricate shape of his daughter Ellen's ear. "My eye came to rest on the delicate convolutions of her ear . . . The thought passed through my mind: 'No, those ears were not created by any chance coming together of atoms in nature.'"[84] This observation instantly produces the thought of design and, hence, of a designer at odds with party orthodoxy. The random combination of molecules and chance generation of life could no longer suffice for Chambers. One senses that this recondite thought in the mind of a committed Communist escalated into an unavoidable clarity. This step towards belief in God proved foundational for Chambers in both thought and act. Chambers defined its importance as challenging another creedal tenet of Communist materialism, " . . . the vision of man's mind displacing God as the creative intelligence of the world. It is the vision of man's liberated mind, by the sole force of its rational intelligence, redirecting man's destiny."[85] Such clarity led Chambers to venture ruin rather than serve Communism. The most obvious fruit of this choice was Alger Hiss's conviction in 1950 for two counts of perjury in connection with testimony he gave to a grand jury concerning his past relationship with Chambers. The conviction for perjury implied the larger unofficial charge of espionage against Hiss for his actions at the State Department on behalf of the Soviet Union.

Chambers's Weary Resolve

St. Augustine instructed that our love is our weight, best exemplified by the overwhelming remorse he experienced at the death of his beloved mother, Monica. If so, the weight of Chambers's love was directed towards liberating men from the worship of ideological gods. The immense weight of this love repeatedly pulled Chambers to earth. Chambers went forward to "give the children of men a slightly better, only slightly better, chance to fight a battle already largely foredoomed."[86] Still, Chambers was unconvinced at the outset of the Hiss trial that his witness would provide a substantive awakening amongst Americans of the dangers of Communist ideology and aggression. One of several instances of tension, if not contradiction, in Chambers's thought was that he continually saw world events as unstoppable forces incapable of direction by men. And yet Chambers held tightly to the dignity of his personal response to evil, a dignity unbowed even in failure and, perhaps, death. Chambers reported to Buckley that "against the clear and forceful evidence of my own mind, I will always give my body to be burned if, by so doing, our children are given even that slightly better chance against the falling night."[87] Standing apart from his contemporaries, Chambers carried their blindness and weakness, to his own detriment, in hope of a more faithful age.

Chambers never found abiding peace in his sacrifice offered at the altar of late modernity. His last letter to Buckley spoke with finality: "Weariness, Bill—you cannot yet know literally what it means. I wish no time would come when you do know, but the balance of experience is against it."[88] Chambers concluded that such weariness was the result of being hit with the runaway freight train of the twentieth century. There was no triumph in Chambers's witness, no moment of terminal victory, only the knowledge that in the historical hour placed upon him he had lived to plan and made his sacrifice.

One, however, must be circumspect in his judgment of Chambers's pessimism. If love is our weight, Chambers's love for God, family, country, and Western civilization was sustained by his own incomplete dialogue with hope, a most difficult virtue. Even when we possess a slight piece of the reality hoped for, thus instantiating it in our experience, we are still blown back by our own finitude. Human limitedness brings no end of anxiety and this fact is never truer than when greatness is placed upon one. This was the burden Chambers carried.

CHAPTER TWO

THE TOTAL CRISIS

IN THE ESSAY "MORNINGSIDE" CHAMBERS illustrated the concept he termed the "total crisis" by pointing to the Bolshevik overthrow of the nascent, republican government in Moscow during the October Revolution of 1917.[1] Chambers's analysis must be carefully parsed, for as he consistently observed, the Bolshevik revolution and the growth of Communist ideology were not the cause of the total crisis. Rather, the total crisis itself was the precondition to such civilization-altering thought and action as observed in Lenin's march to dominance. Chambers understood the total crisis to be the loss of faith in God along with man's failing ability to reason, as theorized and practiced in the rich legacy of premodern Western thought. The eruption of the total crisis was both consequence and cause of the denatured self of late modernity. Unable to dwell in the exponential possibilities of meaning now open to him by this failure of faith and reason, the commitment to ideology became man's own liberation. The heroic quest for an autonomist liberty, richly envisioned by more noble souls of the Enlightenment, had transpired in a far different manner. Under the dispensation of the total crisis, unfailing confidence in a positivist reason—adumbrated as it was by jarring advances in science, technology, and medicine—led man to commit his mind and person to the perfection of existence, one now conceived to have no limits.

Chambers described the Bolshevik revolution in Russia as one that brutally proceeded under the direction of its leaders, Anton Antonov-Avseënko, Leon Trotsky, and Vladimir Ilyich Lenin. The masses provided the onrush of support crucial to the actual takeover of Moscow and the national government and, thereby, framed the prototype for revolution in the twentieth century. The Bolshevik coup was more than a particular display of revolutionary violence. As Chambers noted, "For Antonov-Avseënko and his ragged troops had stormed more than the Winter Palace of the Tsars. They had stormed the Winter Palace of the human mind."[2] Herein was the central element of the story: a revolution led by intellectuals, with heft provided by large masses of men, had set the course for the modern West. This is where the total crisis, as far as Chambers was concerned, approached its fulfillment.

Symbolic of the Western mind's listlessness, "the Winter Palace of the human mind" was a phrase employed by Chambers to demonstrate that the Sovietization of Russia could be the penultimate step in freedom's elimination in the West. The phrase implied that the West, having abandoned the ideals and spirit that formed it, would be unable to measure the catastrophic scope of change in the vitalistic Communism of the Bolsheviks. Moreover, the Communist transformation of the Russian government signaled that history in the twentieth century would be determined by the struggle for the control of the masses.[3] This revolution took varying forms in other states. According to Chambers, the form that emerged in the United States came under the New Deal, while in Britain it took the form of democratic socialism, and in Spain it materialized as falangism.[4] The political upheavals in Western democracies, Chambers believed, were directed by the socialist ideal and its commands for the masses: "each was a form of the same revolution, in different terms, in different stages—the revolution of the masses in the intellectual and physical conditions of the twentieth century."[5]

On the opening page of *Witness* Chambers wrote that upon leaving Communism he told his wife, "You know, we are leaving the winning world for the losing world."[6] Summarized by Chambers as the outcome of two world wars that shattered Europe, the total crisis was not caused by Communism or its "administrative apparatus," the Soviet Union. Communism was merely the feverish symptom of a much larger cancerous growth within Western Civilization. Chambers's view of the total crisis hinged upon the refusal by many to maintain and build on the West's ancient faiths in classical wisdom and biblical faith.

For Chambers, faith encompasses a vision of man understood apart from late modernity and its atomistic individualism, materialism, and corrosion of belief in eternal possibilities and meaningful human action. The rejection of the traditional Western vision of man under God inevitably provided the opportunity to believe that man's mind could determine man's destiny. This was the true cause of the total crisis: the rootless modern—the voracious self-norming individual—stripped bare by rationalism, found his deliverance from the slaughter-bench of history in Communist ideology. Contained in the revolutionary vision was the notion that positivist reason and its modern accomplishments in science and technology could finally eliminate the chaos that frequented man's existence.

If man, as Marx contended, was a part of nature and possessed the rational capability to direct and perfect his destiny by mind alone, then entirely new possibilities for human existence were open.[7] In Chambers's terms, this was an attempt at "a molecular rearrangement of the human mind" promising to extricate man from his position as a tragic figure laboring and suffering under imperfect conditions. While reason was operative in a pre-Marxian conception, it was a reason used by man to discover the laws governing his existence, both limiting it and ennobling it. The reason utilized by Communism was delimited; man possessed the exclusive ability to order his existence and achieve the perfection he desired. Herein lay Communism's profound appeal, in particular to educated elites who discovered again the sheer joy of faith: the power to hold convictions and act on them.[8]

The death of old gods and ideals required man to find new verities to supply belief and illumination in his life. Man had once again the task of locating himself within a structure of meaning. As mentioned previously, the dynamic advances of science and technology, which changed and redirected traditional and ancient forms of existence, seemed the most promising substitute when combined with Marxist theorizing. As part of its ideology, Communism embraced the stunning achievements of scientific civilization, and promised an array of ever extending advancements accomplished by the levers of state power that directed and funded science and scientists. There was also the creeping suspicion, seemingly confirmed in achievements like the *Sputnik* launch, that the material capabilities and promises of Western capitalism were more achievable in the command-control state. Similarly, and importantly for Chambers, by sharing the same belief in the transformative power of science, to the exclusion of any notion of human mystery and human limits, the West implicitly reached across the ideological divide and accepted a kindred materialism.

Chambers reasoned that the philosophical materialism of Communism was the silent edge the ideology held over the old, dying West.[9] On this score, Chambers's analysis was consistent with his overall rendering of the source and conflict in the total crisis. Communism's philosophical materialism was its ideological edge precisely because of the spiritual evacuation that had already largely occurred in the West. The methodological atheism that informally guided the modern West may have objected to Communism, but could not explicate why in a fashion compelling to the hearts and minds of Westerners and, significantly, to those living under Communist rule. In the vast crevasse that opened in the West with the death of God, clear propositions were offered by a vision calling man to a perfected end in abandonment and devotion to ideological Marxism.

Inherent in man's alienation from God is the renunciation of the *preambula fidei* (preambles of the faith) that make even reason itself possible. Such conditions see man as a unity of body and soul with a *telos,* natural and supernatural. Reason and free will show that man is created in *Imago Dei* (Image of God) yet suffused with anxiety, deep-seated error, and sin. Moreover, man experiences himself as a being of love and creativity, but also as one who will know loss, suffering, and frustration.[10]

Man's animality communicates a severe limitedness, while his abilities to reason, engage in abstraction, and will his choices towards preferred ends, provide intimations of awe-consuming power. The existence of finite-infinite contradictions within man results in his interminable conflict.[11] Communism, in Chambers's view, found in the early twentieth century this religiously inspired anthropology largely vanquished in the Western mind and in its centers of political and intellectual power, leaving the West open for a new grand narrative of man's significance and destiny.[12]

Man's impulse to overleap his finitude and fallibility, finally laying hold on a type of perfection, is a perpetual temptation to men.[13] Chambers frequently repaired to Aeschylus' *Prometheus Bound* to explain humanity's recurrent notions of outstripping its natural boundaries.[14] Much like Prometheus, man desires release from his mortal predicament to move above the sovereignty given him, in a manner similar to Prometheus jettisoning the proper sphere allotted him as a god when he attempts to relieve man of his limits. Such desires press upon man when he believes there are no rational limits to his being. Indeed, Communism raised the tenor by proposing that the boundaries man experiences exist because reason and modern science are not employed in circumventing them. Formerly experiencing himself as a displaced being, but with the reconciliation provided by Christian theology, man, in the service of a willed perfection, elevates the disciplines of science, government, and economics to a status of cosmic importance.

Salvation by technique mounts to a creedal belief in man's new formulation of existence.

The new rite of materialism, although unacknowledged by the West as such, made an underlying affinity between the West and the Soviet Union possible.[15] Stripped of its Jerusalem, the West now slouched towards its own Moscow, under the shadow cast by Communism's vision of man over God. Interestingly, Chambers believed it was this affinity that partially explained the disquiet that erupted in America during the Hiss trial. At a certain level both civilizations—one, as a matter of identity and belief, the other through unconscious assumption—were largely involved in the same project of consummating man's existence in the terrestrial sphere. This commonality of materialism not only created sympathy across the ideological divide, but also prevented clear-sighted recognition in the West of the crux of Communism and the dominion it sought to exercise.[16]

The Survival of the West

According to Chambers, the total crisis opened two possible resolutions to the West. The first and fatal conclusion—the one Chambers held more probable, if not inevitable—was the triumph of the Soviet Union and its ideology over the West through military or political defeat, or both.[17] The second conclusion was that the West would defeat Communism, but would assume much of its form.[18] Reasoning in Hegelian terms, as he did on many occasions, Chambers articulated that the struggle required to defeat Communism would prove so overwhelming to the West that it would inevitably incorporate significant features of Communism.[19] In Chambers's view, as the West pushed against Communism it would find itself resembling the imprints of the Communist vision as a necessity to survival. Victory over Communism, under this analysis, entailed a life on terms largely supplied by Communism. The singular elements of Western life—religion, liberty, and culture—would be flattened by the synthesis of the two conflicting systems. Chambers held that the Western inability, or refusal, to define a positive appeal to the Communist world of the West's own genuine beauty and truth contributed to the second conclusion. Bereft of an external claim to goodness and truth, the West could only resolve the total crisis by assuming, in its collective understanding and political organization, the significant features of Communism: a directed economy, highly centralized and overbearing political authority, sparse personal liberty, and law as an ideological weapon.[20] Either option held no appeal to Chambers.

The third possible conclusion, although Chambers resisted calling it that, was that the West, in its struggle with Communist ideology, would discover through suffering the former intellectual, religious, and moral resources that had shaped it into a unique civilization of liberty. In this scenario, Chambers argued there was a way, dispensed by suffering, that the West could recover its essential goodness and vindicate itself against Communism. It could be called the victory option, but it was highly unlikely for several reasons, primarily because it required enormous costs for those willing to pursue it.

One best understands Chambers's rather distressing analysis of the options open to the West by taking a view from the East. For those Eastern Europeans suffering under the weight of Stalinism midway through the twentieth century, the allure of the West must have been profoundly dispiriting, made doubly so by the West's abnegation of the region when its leaders consented to Soviet control. The United States and the British Empire consigned the citizens of the Eastern European states to slavery under Stalin's Russia without consulting them or considering their rights as persons requiring freedom. The conditions created by the virtual enslavement of the Soviet Bloc states afforded its citizens a peculiar vantage point for sizing up the West. Chambers believed that the West was free merely because it had not yet been conquered by Communism, and he asserted that the Easterners were surely nonplussed by the interplay of Communist statecraft and the irresolute West, who, as a matter of policy, refused to directly challenge Communism, morally, politically, or militarily.[21]

Of course, the realist might easily dissect Chambers's analysis by noting the numerous efforts of American presidential administrations during the Cold War to contain and frustrate the Soviet Union's enterprising foreign policy. Even as Chambers published essays on the failure of America and the West to confront the Soviet Union, Harry Truman constructed the intelligence and military offensive capabilities that served American efforts against Communism. Dwight Eisenhower repeatedly utilized the capabilities of the intelligence services to topple governments, harass foreign political leaders, and lend support to center-right and anti-Communist political parties in various states. Contrary to Chambers's articulation of an America lacking nerve and direction in the fight against international Communism, America marshaled resources—from George Kennan's prescient "X Telegram" and the Marshall Plan, to the orchestration of numerous military coups and other precise uses of hard power—in a coherent manner against international Communism from the beginning of the Cold War.

The fact that these efforts were in operation, however, should not obscure or even contradict Chambers's larger point that the enormous power imbalances of America *vis-à-vis* the Soviet Union in the immediate postwar period provided tragically unrealized opportunities for more fruitful attacks and defensive measures against the international Communist project. Chambers believed that the moral and philosophical blindness of leaders in the West was central to this failure. Chambers scorched the Roosevelt Administration's failure to shore up the forces of the Chinese Nationalist leader, Chiang Kai-Shek.[22] In this view, China's ultimate fall to Maoist forces had roots in the New Dealers' failure to comprehend and act prudently against ideological Communism.

According to Chambers, President Eisenhower's strategic problems stemmed from the failure to imagine an anti-Communist foreign policy that relied on more than the ultimate threat of nuclear missiles. While such a strategy had issued into a *stasis* that held together an uneasy peace, a more strategic opportunity was missed because it ignored the intellectual and moral appeal of Communism to states with neutral or large sympathetic populations to Communism.[23] The Communist International, which operated by employing mass intellectual and political conversions independent of any balance of forces, was ignored. Content with the large power imbalances of America's missile arsenals relative to the Soviet Union, Eisenhower and other political leaders let slip needful opportunities for a metaphysical framing of the conflict against the Soviets. The Cold War's version of "the battle for hearts and minds" in America, Chambers noted, punted its opportunities to advance the cause of the West. More distressing to Chambers was that the West punted because it had forgotten its own animating purpose and destiny.

In the wake of producing its own nuclear weapons and by virtue of its massive ground forces, the military power of the Soviet Union reached parity with America and its allies within a few years after World War II. Soviet power, however, had not initially advanced by means of weapons. Chambers found the locus of power in the Soviet Union exclusively in the ideational commitments forged by Communist ideology. The ascendancy of Communism through the Soviet Union had never proceeded directly by strategic Soviet assessments of its possession or lack of hard power. Rather, it progressed by conversions of minds and wills through articulation of the ideological necessity of its vision. Only in the West were international relations theorists and political leaders confused by—and insistent upon downplaying—the ideological motivations to Soviet power.[24]

In Chambers's view America, the commercial and military power of the world, was incapable of gauging the actions of an ideology that once again gave men reasons for hope, belief, and action. Chambers defined his position well in the essay "The Direct Glance":

> For the war of Communism with the rest of mankind is
> first of all a war of ideas. In that war, Communism rejects
> few means of any kind, or none (its system of ideas justi-

fies this practice). But its first assault is always upon the minds of men; and it is from the conversion of minds that it advances to the conquest of mass bodies and their living space. Each advance enables Communism to expedite conversion by political control since, for those whom it controls, Communism has become the one reality. The West (whatever value the captive may give that word) becomes at most a hope, but a hope that has been defeated (that is why the captives are captive); and it is a hope continuously deferred. Hope deferred not only maketh the heart sick; it stirreth profound suspicions that there is something radically wrong with it. In this case, it stirs a suspicion that exactly to the degree that Communism is felt to be evil and monstrous in its effects, there must be something organically wrong with the West that is unequal to prevailing against a power so conspicuously condign.[25]

In this same essay Chambers reiterated his idea that Communism had a magnetic pull on the modern mind. By the assertion of "a purpose and a plan" comparable to a "hurricane or flood" Communism was able to "feed a will to victory."[26] While the West focused on the tangible effects and consequences of its struggle with the Soviet Union it remained oblivious to understanding that the fight at the physical level was, in large measure, already determined by forces more momentous in the region of the human spirit. In 'The Direct Glance" Chambers highlighted the definitive feature of Soviet Communism underneath the appearance of its vast military power: "It promotes not only a new world. It promotes a new kind of man. The physical revolutions which it once incited and now imposes, and which largely distract our attention, are secondary to this internal revolution which challenges each man in his mind and spirit."[27] Communism, even though it relied on a materialistic understanding of man and the unfolding of time, gained adherents owing to its proclamation of truths that found fertile soil in the souls of both Easterners and Westerners.

Going beyond the simplistic analysis of many American anti-Communists, Chambers never charged his nation's leaders with possessing overt sympathy to Communism. Rather, the Western leaders were unable to understand an enemy who pursued immanent ends with transcendent fervor due to their own paucity of spirit. As a comparative device, Chambers connected the rise of Communism in the modern world to the rise of Christianity in the Roman world as projects of psychological and spiritual transformation which had universal impacts.

The transformation Christianity achieved in the early Church was replicated, analogically, by Communism, although accompanied by nuclear weapons, inhumane industry, and totalitarian political power. To illuminate his broader observation on Western bafflement at Communist action, Chambers quoted a letter from the Roman historian Pliny to the Emperor Trajan, whereby Pliny expressed his discontent with the Christians: "From their dirt, their lousiness, their mendacity, they argue with conviction that they are called to redeem the world."[28] Pliny's puzzlement at the early Christians' belief in their divine call to redeem the world can also be viewed as an expression of the inability of any Roman school of thought, or cultural and religious narrative of that particular era, to counter the crucifixion narrative of Christianity. Likewise, the West, after two catastrophic world wars and its movement away from the theological notions that formed its own cult, was unable to grapple with the philosophical and political appeals of Communism.

Chambers believed that the West's primary responses to Communism, as practical as they were ineffectual, were the outcome of the West flexing or appealing to the only form of power it still recognized: material strength. Missing from the Western response to Communism was an entreaty that could fully engage the moral imagination of Easterners and Westerners of the misanthropic depravity of Communism and the totalitarian state. Yet when Chambers asked, "What is the philosophy of the West?" the apparent answers were hidden, or no longer true, and had to be recovered.[29] Chambers said, "In a war for men's minds, what is it that we are offering whose inherent force is so compulsive that it instantly seizes on the imagination of men and incites them to choose it in preference to Communism?"[30] The offering had to be compelling, Chambers's believed, because "incalculable suffering" was inevitable if Communism was to be overthrown.

Chambers's pessimism—or realism, as the case may be—intervened in his attempt to answer what the West should offer the subjects of the "Communist Empire." Although Chambers returned to a full consideration of the role Christianity might play in forming a rallying cry for the West, he initially dismissed it as a unifier, because it had not been proposed as the bridge between oppressed Christians in the East and those in the West.[31] The absence of such an appeal was made more remarkable by the suppression and elimination of Christianity in the Soviet Empire with little resistance or evident concern from the West. Moreover, the West's denial of Communism's inherent evil supported Chambers's judgment. If the West, itself drifting into skepticism and indifference, was unable to see the putrid nature of Communism, then Western churches would be similarly hobbled in their understanding of the Christians' plight in Eastern Europe.

The Telos of Liberty

Liberty, as commonly understood by the West since the Enlightenment, was another logical banner to proclaim to those underneath Communist rule. Chambers admonished, however, that liberty, at this historical juncture, was an idea found wanting by many in both the East and the West. Breaking with the modernist notion of liberty as an extended exercise in autonomy, Chambers's view of liberty was rooted in classical philosophy, leading him to argue that certain conditions were required for its existence to be intelligible and possible.[32] If Western liberty was merely "a political reading of the Bible" then this implied certain necessities: belief in God, the human soul, and intrinsic human freedom.

Chambers thought that these guaranties of freedom had been dismissed by the West and that this dismissal underlay its irrational responses in World Wars I and II and towards the Nazi and Stalinist death camps. Liberty's veracity, no longer seen as possible or compelling, was diminished.[33] In the face of such carnage, Western man had turned towards principles more fitting to his condition within modernity.

Even in America the preservation of freedom, as a norm to guide the actions of government, was under constant drubbing by the policies of progressive taxation, centralized solutions to economic growth, and "managerial capitalism," among others. Chambers excoriated his own country and other free states for their constant diminishment of individual freedom: "The satellite populations can look westward and see that individual freedom is constantly being whittled down in the West in the interest of centralizing government, and they are perfectly competent to infer that this is the result of the . . . same . . . factors that have destroyed their own freedom."[34] Chambers saw that those facing the prospect of being ground by tank treads know their fate clearly and must have been appalled at the spectacle of the West, the same West whose "failure fixed their fate on them" at Yalta.[35]

In defining the message the West could offer those living under Communism, Chambers dismissed any notion of vindicating the West solely by the chauvinistic assertion of military and economic power. The answer was to be found in a return to the beginning, by the recovery of truths forgotten by the modern world. Without such recovery, our meaning and purpose were inherently senseless; thus, liberty was feckless. Through understanding the soul's need for freedom, Chambers proposed a thicker consideration of the rationales for liberty than those typically relied upon by the theorists of modern liberalism.[36]

Chambers held that human life should not be seen as a set of ceaseless attempts to contractually secure one's widest circumference of choice without the consideration of proper ends. Man does not achieve happiness by guaranteeing for himself the widest distance possible from others. In this understanding the end of liberty becomes choice itself, realized in the absence of coercion.

However, choice and coercion, separated from any content that had previously defined the good life, were incapable of definition. The universe Chambers defined and acted upon was one of divine creation that afforded a ground and purpose to man's actions and the opportunities for such freedom to be heroic, dastardly, or more likely, mediocre.

Chambers recognized that the old paths, best reflected in the heritage of classical and Christian thought, no longer seemed to serve man. Of course, the actual consequence of this was not a resigned passivity or fatalism but a frenetic lashing about for purpose and personal definition. Chambers believed that if old narratives no longer sufficiently answered man's existential anxiety he would not cease from enacting meaning in his life for it is an inelastic need, but rather he "will break new paths, though they must break their hearts to do it."[37] Chambers sensed that man "will burst out somewhere, even if such bursting out takes the form of an aberration. For to act in aberration is more like living than to die of futility, or even to live in that complacency which is futility's idiot twin."[38] The emerging theme is that man will strike against his despair. Modern man realizes that he is free to act, even if such action leads to profound woe.

Suffering became pivotal to Chambers's understanding of a life rightly lived, and proved the sure accompaniment to man in serving both liberty and truth. Inextricably linked to a proper understanding of liberty and truth is the recognition of suffering as the inescapable element of man's condition. The embrace of suffering quickly proves nonsensical if one is not prepared to exercise liberty on behalf of truth and to recognize the consequences that may issue from such action. If truth is merely the construction of will, or the outcome of dialectical material forces at work, then suffering becomes futile, a sign of resigned purposelessness. Resulting from the severance of liberty and truth is the relativity of human action ultimately issuing into man pursuing nothing more than the pleasure of his own ego.

Implicit in Chambers's anthropology is the notion of man as servant, never wiser than at the point where he comprehends his fundamental humility. Far from being the legislator of the world, man discovers his meaning subject to the unpredictability of existence. The dignity of the person is therefore located in the freedom of human action directed towards and by a body of truth. Further informing Chambers's understanding of man's conscience and freedom is the deepening of both by the Christian religion. On this score, Chambers offered the following eloquent phrases:

> For it is by the soul that, at the price of suffering, we can break, if we choose, the shackles that an impersonal and rigid Fate otherwise locks upon us. It was the genius of Christianity to whisper to the lowliest man that by the action of his own soul he could burst the iron bonds of Fate with which merely being alive seemed to encase him. Only, it could never be done except at a price, which was suffering. It was because Christianity gave meaning to a suffering endured in all ages, and otherwise senseless, that it swept the minds of men.[39]

Christianity and the supernatural meaning imparted by it now connect the constants of man's life: liberty, truth, and suffering, in a previously unimaginable way. Suffering, under the Christian dispensation, is the way to uncover humane truths dismissed and forgotten in the current age.

Exemplifying Chambers's contention of the strife necessary to achieve victory in the total crisis were the counterrevolutionary actions of the people in Poland and Hungary. The immediate hopelessness in the face of the Soviet Union's monstrous military and political power deployed against their uprisings in 1956 added meaning and valor to their resistance. In their struggles, the Hungarians and Poles had looked westward for assistance but none was forthcoming. For Chambers, Western support did not need to be a muscular response of weapons and material. Instead, the West needed to show firm allegiance and sympathy for the spirit guiding the counterrevolutionaries of '56. In reality, however, the West did nothing.

Chambers' noted in his reflections on the resistance in Poland and Hungary that the West was, perhaps, incapable of meeting either revolt with comprehension or physical support. He opined:

> The real anti-communists are in the satellites. They are materialists, too. But it may be that circumstances will evolve in them a new blend that goes beyond the materialist limit. It is in this sense, and scarcely in any other, that I tend to agree with [James] Burnham that the historical crux lies in Poland, etc. Here, and, in time, farther east, something restorative may develop. Look as I will, I can

find no signs of anything like that in the West, and it is
this spiritual (and intellectual) deadness that invests the
current crisis with that numbing sense of: so what?[40]

Lurking in Chambers's interpretation of the Polish and
Hungarian uprisings was the interplay of forces inherent in the
total crisis. In this context, aggression by the Soviet Union, if not
countered in a vigorous and imaginative manner, spelled that
the West was largely devoid of the energy necessary to preserve
its civilization.[41] A rebalance of forces was being augured by the
peoples of Hungary and Poland who attempted to recover their
liberty and "meaning." The post-war advance of the Soviet Union
in Eastern Europe was now finally being met by the most direct,
if doomed, countervailing response. As Chambers put it, "At the
moment, the Poles are making history. The West is making politics. . . . The difference is between a creative act and pettifoggery.
What is opening on the Polish plain is a new phase of history, a
new thrust of the spirit."[42] Thus, the "pettifoggery" or trifling over
relatively insignificant details of Western politics only saw an array
of proposed "realist" limitations to decisive efforts against Soviet
Communism. Prominent in Chambers's seemingly pessimistic
position amidst these uprisings was the lack of a "sense of destiny,"
or purposeful thinking and action by those charged with defending
freedom against tyranny.

The counterrevolutionary movements in Poland and Hungary
were something of a sign of hope for Chambers. If the West was
unsure of itself and of Communist intentions, the peoples of these
states held to no such illusion:

In the absence of any other effective force, there has now emerged, on the Polish and on the Hungarian plains, another force, pathetic in its physical impotence and inequality, but heroic in its purpose which has challenged both the morally empty West and the corrupt Communist power in which, hitherto, destiny has inhered. This is the dialectic force of the revolution itself, creating, out of its own inner conflict, a new force of destiny to counteract and challenge the older force, which corruption has long made into a fiendish masquerade of fated force.[43]

Here, Chambers highlighted his prominent theme of the strange victory offered the sufferer in man's opposition to the inhumane force of the ideological regime. The West may have a measure of peace and separation of distance through its prosperity and military capability, but its own sure fate silently smothered its nobler, former spirits. In time, through the unwinding of the political and philosophical dialectic of Communism the West, too, may realize a similar subjugation.

After the end of the 1956 Polish and Hungarian uprisings Chambers remarked:

I say that what makes us all sick with a sickness we cannot diagnose is that, in the current crisis, the West has gained the world (or thinks it has), but has lost its own soul. I say: the Poles and the Hungarians have lost the world (or whatever makes it bearable—they live in Hell), but they have gained their own souls. What price, Power without purpose? Dulles mouthing moralities while on the streets of Budapest children patrolled the shattered housefronts, with slung rifles and tormented faces. I say those children, whatever their politics, will have grown to men while Dulles and his tribe lie howling. . . . [44]

Poland's stouthearted resistance in 1956 returned three decades later to begin the great unraveling of the Soviet Empire under the leadership of men decisively on the side of the human spirit. In light of the inspiration provided by the witness of John Paul II and Lech Walesa, and the willingness of Polish citizens to resist their Soviet masters in the last decade of the Soviet imperium, Chambers was proved correct when he intuited in 1956 that a new force "heroic in its purpose" exploded in Poland. To Chambers, however, this heroic purpose was not present in the West, and contributed to its continuing downfall.

The devastating consequence flowing from Western failure of nerve was the accommodation of the Soviet Union and many of its tactics.[45] Such accommodation was insanity to Chambers, which he believed fueled the notion of the Soviet Union's inevitability.[46] Adding to Chambers's disbelief was the intrinsic corruption in Communism and its sheer murderous reality, which led him to conclude that "it is insane that the rest of the world could co-exist with, and largely connive at, such insanity."[47] The world's inaction and acceptance of criminal Communism pointed to no other acceptable conclusion other than its own sickness.

Courage and the Crisis

In "Letter to My Children," Chambers detailed the utter ruin of his quite remarkable and successful journalism career as one of several deplorable consequences that arose from his testimony against Alger Hiss.[48] *Time* remained loyal to Chambers for a short interval after his accusations against Hiss were leveled, but facing intense pressure from a combination of senior journalists and outside interests, editor Henry Luce eventually ended Chambers's tenure at the magazine. Chambers's position as senior editor of *Time* afforded him a handsome salary and a prominent platform to controvert Communism. It is fair to ask, then, why Chambers would sacrifice his career to turn informant against Alger Hiss.

As a courier for the Fourth Section of Soviet Military Intelligence Chambers delivered United States government documents received from Alger Hiss and other underground apparatus members to agents of the Soviet government. Chambers the defector saw that these former actions committed as an agent of the Soviet Underground equated to an existential debt he was obligated to redeem by becoming an informant. The demand of such debt was intensely personal, but also corporate in its transitive effects on American society. A debt made exponentially worse, Chambers believed, by the fact that such espionage was still being conducted with little or no abatement.

Heavily factoring into Chambers's calculations to become an informant was the example provided by Walter Krivitsky, an ex-Communist and former head of the Fourth Section of Soviet Military Intelligence in Western Europe. Chambers met and con-

versed with Krivitsky at length shortly after the announcement of
the Nazi-Soviet Non-Aggression Pact of 1939.[49] Having defected to
the United States, Krivitsky lived in rural upstate New York and
believed (accurately) that he and his family were under constant
surveillance by Soviet Intelligence. During an all-night conference,
Krivitsky detailed to Chambers the brilliant logic, from the Communist position, of the Non-Aggression Pact.[50] From Moscow's angle
the Non-Aggression Pact, which guaranteed nonviolence between
the Soviet Union and the German Reich, was justified given that
its imperialist purposes were substantially advanced by the divisions
within the West that would be created by the Pact. This political
logic, which Chambers reported he missed until uncovered by
Krivitsky, resonated with him beyond geopolitical theorizing. The
world that Chambers left at the age of twenty-four under the notion
that it was irreparably doomed, and to which he had returned as an
ex-Communist, was fatally threatened by twinned barbaric powers.[51]

The grotesque alliance between the world's two reigning
totalitarian powers in the Non-Aggression Pact presented striking
confirmation to Chambers of the forces arrayed against Western
Europe and the United States. Hitler's invasion of Poland could
now happen without regard for Soviet reaction. At the same time,
the Soviet Union could partition select parts of Eastern Europe and
the Baltic states. The monstrous events of 1939 propelled Chambers
to add teeth to his counterrevolutionary status and finally become
an informant against Communist espionage within the United
States government.[52]

The total crisis had reached a new definitive stage with the
Nazi-Soviet Pact and the impending war that could end in world

control by the totalitarian states. Moreover, Chambers held a personal connection to the Non-Aggression Pact, as confirmed by Krivitsky: United States intelligence documents Chambers had been responsible for as an underground courier were likely to be delivered to Berlin.[53] Now made inevitable by the Non-Aggression Pact, the oncoming world war convinced Chambers to divulge his knowledge of Communist espionage within the United States government to Assistant Secretary of State, Adolf A. Berle.[54]

Chambers visited Adolf A. Berle with New York journalist Isaac Don Levine in 1939 and revealed the full contents of the Soviet Union's Washington underground operations as he understood them.[55] Chambers's first strike at Communist underground activities, however, did not prove particularly fruitful. While the depth of Chambers's revelations surprised Berle, and were incapable of being dismissed, accused individuals were not sequestered from official government duties, nor was any substantial investigative and enforcement activity pursued by Berle.

His disclosures to Berle having been substantially ignored, Chambers spent World War II from his editorial stoop at *Time* learning to produce and eventually master the journalistic style of condensing and shaping intellectual, cultural, and political events into the appealing and consumable form that Henry Luce craved. Chambers's feared version of events that he adopted from Krivitsky had proven partially accurate in the wake of World War II. The West, initially split by divergent interpretations of geopolitical facts, not to mention the contrasting efforts of various political leaders and political trends, had joined to defeat the German military machine. Krivitsky's prediction of a divided West that would hesitate before Soviet aggression proved true as allied euphoria faded in the post-war period. The Soviet Union was crucial to the West's military efforts in overcoming Nazism and was perhaps even more ideologically dedicated to destroying persons, groups, and states that posed obstacles to its progress than the Third Reich. This was observed early in the post-war period by the Soviet Union's tyrannical hold on the Eastern European states. Chambers, along with other thinkers on the American Right, came immediately to the position that the chief result of World War II was not peace but perpetual conflict with the Soviet Union.

Chambers dramatized the foregoing stance through a short story *Time* printed in 1945 immediately following the Yalta Conference entitled "Ghosts on the Roof."[56] Giving the piece additional audacity was the media blackout that governed Yalta while "The Big Three" made decisions that affected the fates of millions of people. The story proceeds as a conversation between the ghosts of the Tsar Nicholas, the Tsarina Alix, and the Muse of History, Clio, while the tsar's five children remain in the background. From the roof of the former ruling family's Livadia Palace, the ghosts observe the Yalta meetings and discourse on Stalin's international political objectives at the conference. While the tsar's ghost is more than slightly disfigured by the gaping bullet hole in his head, he manages to communicate profound admiration for the political-military accomplishments of Stalin.[57] The tsar exclaims, "What statesmanship! What Vision! What power! We have known nothing like it since my ancestor, Peter the Great, broke a window into Europe by overrunning the Baltic states in the Eighteenth century. Stalin has made Russia great again."[58]

In "Ghosts on the Roof" Chambers leveled the Western intellectual consensus that cooperation between the Soviet Union and
the United States in constructing a postwar peace was not just
necessity, but a moment of humanitarian grace leading a shattered
world onto a new plane of international order. Chambers would
have none of it. The piece ends with Chambers's penchant for
isolating perceived bits of Communist strategy and hurling them
at readers whom he believed were likely unaware of the true ends
of Soviet policy. After the tsar lists with enthusiasm the states and
territories conquered by Stalin, Clio describes how enlightened
opinion will receive Yalta:

> But your notions about Russia and Stalin are highly
> abnormal. All right-thinking people now agree that Rus-
> sia is a mighty friend of democracy. Stalin has become a
> conservative. In a few hours the whole civilized world will
> hail the historic decisions just reached beneath your feet
> as proof that the Soviet Union is prepared to collaborate
> with her allies in making the world safe for democracy
> and capitalism. The revolution is over.[59]

Countering Clio, the tsarina informs her that she could not be
more wrong in her charge that Stalin was a friend of the democratic world. Chambers turned the knife further into the bibulous
credulity of Western policy makers when the tsar reminds Clio, the
historical dialectic is more complicated than her "static concepts
of 19th-Century liberalism."[60] To communicate this point more
efficiently, the tsarina explains, "between two systems of society,

which embody diametrically opposed moral and political principles, even peace may be only a tactic of struggle."[61] Three years later *Time* ran the piece again because its central prognostication of Stalin's goals for Eastern Europe had proved highly accurate.[62]

After the combined Allied assault disintegrated the Nazi empire, only two principal powers, the Soviet Union and the United States, and their respective spheres of influence existed. In Chambers's view the loss of reason and faith among its elites handicapped the West's efforts against Communism. The West, therefore, faced not only the external enemy embodied in the Soviet Union and its international capabilities, but also the foe within, or the failures of many in its intellectual class to defend the principles of a free society.

The once formidable political economy of classical liberalism was now an imperiled position. It was with few exceptions—albeit ones that proved significant—dismissed almost entirely by leading lights throughout Western universities and governments. Free markets were viewed as dysfunctional precisely because of the broad scope given to individual and capital initiative. The worldwide economic depression, and its debilitating scarcities of goods and services, contributed greatly to the rationalization of central economic planning, or, at the least, a notion that markets should be actively managed by the state.[63]

Constitutional democracy and the rule of law were problematic because they were incapable of the definitive, positive action required by governments to meet the ever-expanding demands of modern democracy. The centralization of power in the Soviet Union was seen by many as containing substantial teaching opportunities for the direction of modern democratic politics. The egalitarian ideal as enforced by state planning promised more than equal freedom but the abundance of goods and services that were scarce and highly prized by citizens of Western democracies. All this purported beneficence occurred in a state where policy was proclaimed in full by a dictator and central committee. The only limits to law in the Soviet arrangement were the individual wills of Soviet rulers. Inherent in all such misguided praise was the view that the limitations to government power given in a nod to abstract human rights, or the dignity of the person, were the real barrier to full realization of human potential. Western governments had largely abandoned the idea that the people had the power, not the governments, and that rights were checks on governmental abuse, not the circumscription of individual prerogative within the state's unrestrained sphere of total control.

The idea of limited government stumbled horribly in the balance created by the intellectual appeal of political and economic centralization. Although penned before the conclusion of World War II, Chambers's essay "The Revolt of the Intellectuals" was poignant on this rapturous allure of Communism and its rationale of planning to the American literary illuminati. On this score Chambers's observed:

The depression came to them as a refreshing change. Fundamentally skeptical, maladjusted, defeatist, the intellectuals felt thoroughly at home in the chaos and misery of the '30s. Fundamentally benevolent and humane, they loved their countrymen in distress far more than they could ever love them in prosperity. And they particularly enjoyed life when applause began to greet their berating of the robber barons, president makers, economic royalists, malefactors of great wealth.

From this it was but a step to supporting the Communist Party, especially when Marxists pointed out that while under capitalism, a writer is either a wretched hack or a vulgar best seller, under Communism he is a privileged employee of the State.[64]

Chambers pivoted in the essay by concluding that for many fellow travelers, whom he listed by name, the Nazi–Soviet Pact of 1939 had compelled them to get off the Communist train and abandon their ideology in a formal sense. Such abandonment, however, lacked a complete grasp of the ideology's particular darkness. An acquittal was not forthcoming in the essay and remained contingent on "whether the U.S. literary liberals will bring their intelligence to bear effectively on the side of democracy."[65] For Chambers, the total crisis that crossed into its penultimate stage after the conclusion of World War II was always a conflict between the faiths of freedom and Communism.[66]

As detailed earlier in this chapter, in Chambers's writing freedom entailed more than a notion of negative liberty typically found in many British and American writers who challenged political and economic centralization during the twentieth century. Chambers's faith in freedom—while capable of being subjected to rational investigation and hence not an irrational faith—found worthy expression in a series of essays he wrote for *Life* on the

development of ideas, history, and culture in Western Civilization.[67] Here, Chambers revealed the source of his devotion to the
wellsprings of the West that he believed had been buried in the
age of late modernity.

Chambers's essay "The Middle Ages" is suffused with the
notion of freedom as man's possession that is perfected in ennobling
human action rendered through love of God. Tribute is given in the
essay to what Chambers believed were the three foremost achievements of the medieval age: the Gothic cathedral, Thomism, and
Dante's *Divine Comedy,* with all three forms representing man's
need to locate his freedom and dignity in the eternal being. Moreover, Chambers analysis of these three bodies of work demonstrates
his belief that freedom, rightly conceived, emerges best in practice
and obedience to an ideal. The result is an uncovering of beauty
revealing to man the essential goodness of his being that is able,
under certain dispensations, to pierce through the dark glass that
enshrouds so much of his existence.

Chambers focused on the construction of the Gothic cathedral
in the medieval period as an exhibit of the devotion to an ideal
and the working through habit to concretize one's love, which was
"a prayerful uprush of stone" that "medieval man perceived . . .
had magnificently created his need of God in stone."[68] Somewhat
analogous to the medieval theological rendering given by Thomas
Aquinas, the Gothic cathedral was the outcome of supreme love,
arduous effort, and material costs that fully illuminated man within
the hierarchical order of being. Freedom was therefore grounded in
being. Man best understood his greatness through the complementary ordering of being, devotion, and practice. Chambers believed

that the denial of this understanding and its spiritual and practical provisions explained the radically displaced individualism of his era and its logical contribution to the total crisis.

The objection to this notion focuses on its undue constriction of choice. If liberty is authentic only when exercised according to the standard of classical natural law, persons are not really free, bound as they are to choose according to standards dictated to the human conscience. Conscience, however, always remains free to respond and choose. Certain choices will accord more with man's dignity and thus confirm and ennoble him in their objects and goods, other choices alienate man, not only dividing man against himself, but opening to him entirely new realms of unfreedom. The deeper point made by Chambers was the imprint of eternal order on man's soul that led him through his cooperation to the order of a peace only by way of transcendence.

The recovery of such freedom—lost, as it was, through a series of wrong intellectual and political turns—figured prominently in Chambers's writings. Man, who had been seemingly liberated in the modern era, found himself mistaken about his true end. His singular greatness, translated into autonomous control of existence, sought to will perfectionist aims into existence. Of course, what man actually willed became the irreproachable standard of his existence and the definitive criterion by which other men were judged. Thus, the world in the total crisis, laboring under the absence of limits and confused about essential goods, became a world unfit for and hostile to freedom. To regain an authentic liberty one must display a reasoned confidence in man's singular capacity to understand the truth about himself. The knowledge obtained through self-reflection, of the soul reaching beyond itself to the foundation of its existence and rationality, opened again to man the possibility of truth, wisdom, and the ability to be a witness.

CHAPTER THREE

TRAGEDY AND HOPE

WITHIN THE MANY PECULIAR STRAINS of Chambers's writings is a declaration, personal as it is universal, that man must free himself from the rapacious jaws of modern intellectual error and its incredible *pathos.* In the twentieth century, human tragedy would take the form of attempting to rise above the modern postulate that man's mind constitutes reality. The movement up from contemporary gnosticism and the human wonderings that it artificially filled and directed, necessitated pain and suffering. This was to be the real tragedy: in recalling Western man back to his foundations of culture, one invited the agonies resulting from an attempt at authentic liberation. The hope sustaining the endeavor rested with man again understanding the grounding and purpose of his being, one that went beyond the narrative of materialist Communism and its own *preambula fidei.*

On Election Day, 1952, a powerful heart attack felled Chambers, leaving him sprawled on the floor of his local polling location. While convalescing at St. Agnes Hospital in Baltimore Chambers

recorded several of his most notable observations on confinement, loss, pain, and *kénosis* (self-emptying), which amplified
his larger concerns on the attenuated condition of the West. In
these remarks, Chambers offered a painful and, perhaps, inexplicable way to emancipation: suffering. One particular virtue of
his recovery period was the many visits he received from Father
Alan, a Passionist monk. Sharing Chambers's reflective capacity
to travel along the tortuous path of the twentieth century, Father
Alan left an indelible imprint on Chambers, tempering his more
severe reflections on the West.

Chambers, the man who at times proclaimed that he stood
within no religious or political tradition, must have confounded
Father Alan in these conversations. The interesting parallel in their
association, one that remained with Chambers for life, was that
both men—one by express operation as chaplain, the other by self-
directed mission—carried the burden of healing and restoration.
Chambers pointedly asked Father Alan whether he had been right,
substantively and prudentially, to remark in *Witness* that the West
was the "losing side" in its struggle with Communism.[1] Chambers,
then as now, had endured criticism for the remark. He was at odds
with much of the American global experience, not to mention the
growing strength and aggressiveness of anti-Communism within
America. Critics accused him of defeatism and pessimism.

In response to Chambers's inquiry, the monk offered the following question: "Who says that the West deserves to be saved?"[2]
Chambers immediately understood this question to be pointing
towards the Promethean overreach of the West itself, which in
rejecting its central ideals of faith, freedom, and the irreducible

complexity of the human soul, had led to Communism. While the West now sought to extricate itself from Communism, it remained blind to its inability to comprehend its own moribund spirit. Father Alan's question underscored Chambers's larger observation that many in the West failed to comprehend the measure of its moral worth. The difficulty was that the West failed to recognize that Communism was its own creation, the natural offspring of its Enlightenment rationalism. Thus, the criticisms of Chambers's, the "losing side" conception actually served, paradoxically, his larger idea: a West unable to believe in its primary truths could not stand up against the terror of hyper-rationalist ideology.

In Chambers's telling, tragedy consisted in struggle, in the decision to live against the demonic spirit of the age, conscious of an incomprehensible suffering that must follow hard on such a decision. Tragedy visited men who attempt to find truth in and through the deprivations and abuses that constantly befell such efforts.[3] Destruction, failure, and defeat at the hands of more powerful or duplicitous enemies were not tragic, but instead were proof of the endurance of evil. The magnanimous response was the struggle to grasp goodness even when the very object seemed unobtainable. Therefore, tragedy was not in Chambers's exile from journalism, or from respectable membership in society, but in his own awakening and defection from Communism and the subsequent decision to inform against it. In these acts he was the human soul that "awakes and seeks, in suffering and pain, to free itself from crime, violence, infamy, even at the cost of life."[4]

Largely unavoidable, tragedy was a constant in human history. However, it did not complete man's story or terminate in his pity and contempt. Rather, the struggles of tragedies built monuments and pillars to human greatness, the greatness derived from moral choices that exalted beauty and truth. Chambers affirmed that "tragedy has always filled men, not with despair, but with a sense of hope and exaltation."⁵ Such hope derived from the conviction that our lives were not mere repetitions of temporal acts that found and contained no lasting meaning. The purposelessness that pervaded much of the contemporary modern West was the product not of tragedy, but of the denial of goodness, of intelligible essences, in creation and in man, thus making tragedy, as Chambers understood it, obsolete. The inability to believe in one's civilization, in the integrity of its grand narratives and of its justice ended, ineluctably, in apathy and despair.

Prompting these ruminations were the episodes of horror that dotted, or rather engulfed, the political and psychological horizons of the twentieth century, forever altering the West's conception of itself and reality as a whole. Chambers indicated that such episodes demonstrated the helplessness of so many souls before the various incarnations of terror that consumed them. These events entered Chambers's consciousness because he had participated in the clandestine workings of a regime that achieved so many faceless, nameless deaths. He attached this observation of modern ideology's incalculable and enormous suffering to another agonizing thought—namely, that such horror had resisted direct recognition and the consequent need for atonement.

Chambers reflected on two episodes of inexplicable terror and evil that revealed the demented cast of mind that dominated his time. In the first event, known as the Katyn Forest Massacre of

1940, the Soviet Red Army executed well over twenty thousand Polish officers and enlisted soldiers. (International opinion long held that the Nazi government had been responsible for the massacre—a myth perpetuated by Stalin, who had issued the execution order. In 1990 the Soviet Union finally owned up to the murders.)[6] Chambers saw in the event the devastating feature that the free world had considered the liquidation of these soldiers unremarkable.

In conversation with Father Alan, Chambers asked what could be made of this horrific night of slaughter. "Tell me," he said, "if God is a God of Good, why did he permit those simple men to be massacred by that monstrous evil?"[7] Father Alan's response of silence was, Chambers concluded, the only reasonable reply.[8] Both men sensed that the murders in the Katyn Forest were beyond comprehension and rationality. Father Alan's honesty here, along with his prior question implying that perhaps the West was not meant to survive, conveyed to Chambers the surpassing worth of the monk's meditations on evil in the modern predicament. To answer his own question Chambers recalled a passage from one of his favorite novels, Fyodor Dostoevsky's *The Possessed*. "Water the earth with your tears, Shatushka, water it a foot deep with your tears." Chambers added the following gloss to the text: "The other answers do not now matter, because that is perhaps the best answer; or, at least, that is the one we all come to."[9] In the face of modern horror and its sheer mindlessness Chambers and his bedside monk stopped short of inconsolability, but they were fundamentally altered by events so grievous, so wounding, to the communion of persons.

The second event involved the slow, bit-by-bit massacre of allegedly disloyal foreign Communists in Moscow during the Great

Purge.[10] Quartered at Moscow's Hotel Lux, certain prisoners were daily removed from the hotel for eventual liquidation. From this hotel of nightmares, Chambers chose two female German Communists, Alice Abramovitz and Frieda Rubine, to discuss in detail. They were both staying at the hotel when Alice was summoned by authorities.[11] Authorities compelled her to leave her infant child behind, alone. Alice desperately attempted to place the child with other prisoners on her floor, but all refused, because to accept the child was to invite their own deaths. Even Frieda, her closest friend, refused Alice's daughter, shutting her door the moment she saw Alice coming with a host of police agents behind her. Frieda permitted Alice to flail and thrash in a pointless attempt to save her child, and Frieda was unable after the event to forgive herself—or more accurately, as Chambers observed, "she could not endure herself."[12]

The Hotel Lux liquidation, for Chambers, was a moment of wolves at the door devouring both woman and child. The persons most directly involved refused to defend the moral order. But for the soldiers to have resisted performing murder, and their superiors to have acted against directives from higher authorities, would have required heroic virtue, a virtue that Chambers intimated may not have been possible within a totalitarian regime. Having ceded his dignity and authority as a person to the state the individual was no longer capable of exercising the responsibility and judgment needed to resist tyranny. However, for Frieda, or any prisoner, to have taken the child may not have mattered ultimately. Chambers observed that such an act may have only momentarily delayed the relentless state-enforced ideology from devouring another victim.[13]

The underlying connection between the Hotel Lux liquidation and the Katyn Forest Massacre was the profound moral failure of persons—in these cases, soldiers—to question the reality-distorting mechanisms of a regime that murdered human beings. Of course, to question the regime was unthinkable. This prohibition permitted the massive scale of murders in all Communist regimes. The bonds of a humane order were dissolved by the armed ideologies of the modern period. People could not appeal to the crucial elements under attack by the Stalinist regime—conscience, moral order, and the dignity of the human person—even at the last moment before terror owned another person. Chambers recorded that human action in defense of such truths seemed to take on the cast of meaninglessness. This type of action may have serviced another great truth of the modern era: to die in service of nobility is to die for, seemingly, nothing.[14]

For Chambers, the massacres in the Katyn Forest and Hotel Lux met at the intersection of despair. Two groups were extinguished by agents of the Soviet Union acting in the service of an ideology unopposed by the West at that time—that, indeed, many intellectuals actually favored. The question was how one could contemplate these atrocities and act after what had occurred and what was continuing to occur. The character of late modernity along with the enormity of its trepidations seemed to portend hollowness in human action. The remnants of defiance were interior acts of will effecting goodness, despite the odds of defeat.[15] While these two events of mass murder soon became comprehensible to Chambers, his eventual understanding pointed to the almost vanquished ideal that men, in the final analysis, must place themselves in the service of objects of enduring worth. Life, as Chambers's favorite poet Rainer Maria Rilke observed, was one where iron grew, an observation that terror and violence were inevitable, good would give way to evil. However, persons shaped events, no matter how improbable the balance of forces appeared. Man's actions were determined by their moral purpose, even in the many desperate circumstances of the bloody twentieth century.

Chambers's notion of man as an enfleshed being, winged by faith, is more fully understood in the context of his own exodus from ideology, an exodus impelled by the knowledge of terror, but completed by his grasp of the ground of man's being. Moreover, Chambers's inner dialogue on man's existential identity did not occur within the stately halls of a university building, or in abstract theorizing, but in the low decade of the 1930s marked by calamitous events, at home and abroad, almost unfathomable to the comparatively well-adjusted American of present day. None of his existential turns, however, were more ominous or threatening than the question posed by the true logic of Communism, which was undeniably revealed in the Stalinist purges of the 1930s.[16]

The murder of those who had been founding-era revolutionaries of the Soviet experiment was an exercise in evil. The revolution, Chambers observed, was devouring itself. Communism was revealed in its brutal, honest complexity. For, as Chambers reasoned, the murders, while horrific, remained justifiable within the ideological context of Leninist Communism.[17] The revolution needed to mount a higher, more advanced stage of power, an elevation that demanded the elimination of those tied to its former workings. The fulfillment of Lenin's promise now required new leaders—or just one, Stalin. If the Stalinist hold on power became the omnipresent source of blood and destruction in the Soviet Union during the 1930s, the actual liquidation of political opponents was determined by Communism itself and the vision it proposed.

Chambers concluded during this period that Communism was the wellspring of evil, capable of producing millions of dead bodies. This conclusion Chambers reached—of Communism's grisly, dark logic that suffuses the consciences and actions of its adherents, thereby undergirding the murderous extermination of opponents—was a truth many in the West refused to heed. The descent of wisdom into man's mind is never an easy reception, never more true than when intelligible reality overwhelms the prior conceptions one has constructed. In ways both obvious and obscure this particular wisdom that Chambers heard and responded to grated across the minds of many Western intellectuals in his day, and still does in our own. Perhaps the implications of Communism's foundational corruption reached toward truths too unsettling and uncomfortable for the world as constructed by so many intellectuals.

The falsity of Communism likely portends the invalidation of its central metaphysical contention that all reality is material, there is no God. In the absence of God, Communism reigns. Man has become his own artificer. The truth of God and a divine order of being was and remains the truth too horrifying for Communists, socialists, and their contemporary progeny of progressive thinkers to accept. The implication of God's existence is that reality contains truths that cannot be circumscribed by the human mind. These truths of God and man Chambers recognized shortly after he understood the philosophical predicate of Communism's innate barbarity.

Chambers described the intense, soulful turn he experienced after his recognition of Communism's malignant influences as one of an indefinable nature and yet of unmistakable importance.[18] He initially interpreted this intensely internal phenomenon as weakness, as something owing to an inability to complete Communist Party commitments, but he came to realize that it was a spring of hope emerging from the majesty and mystery of being. In correspondence years after the Hiss trial, Chambers recorded that in such moments of substantive reevaluation, of conversion, one groped forward in spite of the known unknowns.[19]

These unknowns are best understood as those puzzling realities facing the revolutionist who must desert his post and begin to stumble forward in a society that does not recognize his philosophical and spiritual achievements. These achievements, forged in the painful extraction from prior ideological traps, go unrecognized by a society and nation seemingly unaware that a confrontation for its soul, and therefore its future, was being clandestinely waged in its government, media, and intellectual centers of power. Chambers the defector would remain anonymous in his conversion—for a while. That others reached to Chambers during this time of gaping need confirmed the other insight Chambers simultaneously began to understand: the soul's logic of love overcomes the logic of mind and reason—the logic before which Communism bowed in awe.

Chambers's description of the particular moment of personal turning from Communism was emblematic of his thinking as a whole: "I knew that my faith, long held and devoutly served, was destroyed long before I knew exactly what my error was, or what the right way might be, or even if there were a right way."[20] His error was, of course, more than intellectual, as it was a subscription to Communism, held to as "the only way out for the 20th century."[21] His lurch forward did not happen by the clean light of any orthodoxy. Guided by the assertion of will, drawn, as it was, by the pull of something abiding that subsisted above "mind, history, or progress," he began his "impossible return." Led forward by an indefinable sense of Providence, Chambers explained this moment by citing Dostoevsky's Shatov who states, in *The Possessed,* "I will believe."[22]

Amidst his total return from Communism, Chambers recalled, "I cannot say that I then believed in God. I sought God. I sought him with the hopeless sense that by finding him I must at once lose what I had scarcely found."[23] Chambers, too, will believe, and as he recorded, "I became what I was. I ceased to be what I was not."[24] The stumbling now came to an end. Shocked by the horror of the ideological enterprise he had served, Chambers, one who inhaled the poisons of the twentieth century as a Communist and traitor to his country, emerged to dispel his confusion and to force one of the most dramatic divisions in American politics and culture.

A Literary Imagination

To better understand Chambers's version of the recrudescence of man, one should return to the beginning of his professional writing career when he was "the hottest literary Bolshevik in America."[25] Chambers wrote a series of short stories in the 1930s for the Communist-controlled literary publication *The New Masses.* The stories remain notable for their attempts to vindicate the individual acting within Communist ideology.[26] Chambers portrayed the Communist "in four basic commitments—in suffering, under discipline, in defeat, in death."[27] Tragedy existed in the inescapability of these realities for the man who chose to live heroically, in spite of such conditions.[28]

Chambers's story "You Have Seen the Heads" received high acclaim in the Communist-literary world. It was performed theatrically on the Bolshevik stage and dramatized the Chinese civil war through the eyes of a remote provincial villager.[29] The unnamed protagonist's village is characterized by defeat and injustice: nationalist tax collectors pillage his fields, the army conscripts him, private lenders fleece him. He is unable to protect his village and his fields, even his own family. The village elder urges him to understand his situation with wisdom and humility rather than fight against it, promising that he will experience a sublime peace by restraining his desire to commit violence.

But Wan gan chi, the protagonist's boyhood friend, and a committed Communist killed by nationalist forces at the story's end, helps him understand their radically unjust situation. Wan gan chi also informs the villager that the elder has been quietly informing on villager resistance to nationalist authorities, ensuring the deaths of many in the village community. Thus the elder's apparent wisdom has meant death for those who listened to it.

Emerging near the end of the drama is Chambers's peculiar sense of tragedy. The protagonist finally registers the injustice he has experienced. In a mode fully Chambersian, he perceives that liberation will not come solely through defeat of his nationalist oppressors: rather, he can achieve true freedom only by releasing himself of the false ideas the village elder has breathed into him. In short, the elder's notion of restraint, understanding, and peace are false compromises in the tyrannical situation that hold the villagers at abeyance, thereby permitting the bourgeois order to inflict starvation and murder. The protagonist's first act of justice is to kill the elder, thus removing the contagion of evil and falsehood.

Here, the Marxist refrain that the wisdom of religion and classical virtue was merely a device used by the propertied classes to soothe the proletariat found its echo. Chambers's teaching, seen in the protagonist's reversal of the elder's advice, augured that wisdom may portend the heightening of conflict, a willingness to be bled white for higher ideals.

The role of the human spirit directing men through perilous situations thrown at them by unjust structures of localized power is central to "You Have Seen the Heads." The crucial element in the protagonist's decision to eliminate the elder is his conscience, which reforges the human goods desecrated by Chinese nationalist authorities and by their quiet accomplice, the elder. If the elder's prior admonition to self-denial carried authority with the hero, relying as it did on the integrity of his conscience, it is this same conscience that now seeks vindication by killing the elder and joining the *Tai i kai* (Communist militia) to begin the work of building a new order. The germ of such an order is located in the protagonist's ending proclamation of Communist resistance: "We are harried among mountains. The march to victory is up the sharp sides of mountains."[30]

The import of the story, relying as it does on the human spirit to inform men in their choices and actions, should have been difficult for many Communists to accept. The tale contains no iron laws of ideology slowly grinding up capitalist opposition. There is not even the explicit appearance of unjust capitalism. Primarily, there is the person, who comes to possess the sheer worth of his being, responding nobly to inhuman actors and forces. That these stories were so well received in Communist circles perhaps indicates the irrepressibility of the human spirit and its ability to receive goodness, indeed truth, despite prior ideological commitments.[31] As Chambers remarked in *Witness,* in every man there always remains "a scrap of soul," allowing him to perceive truths that implicate the human soul, thereby resisting the devastations of ideology.

In Chambers's postexodus short story "The Devil," written for *Time* magazine in 1948, he furthers the notions of defeat and suffering in his understanding of tragedy, to include the loss of love and creativity that the sufferer encounters in his misery.[32] "The Devil" relates a New Year's Eve conversation between a pessimist and the Devil at a New York City nightclub populated by well-heeled patrons and topless dancers. The story begins when the Devil finds the pessimist staring at him and exclaims:

> I do not think that I should stare too long into eyes which, in better times, have borne the inexpressible light of heaven and read their doom by the flocculent night of Hell. Eyes, which, in the dawn of the Creation, have watched with flaming envy as, at the great words, 'Fiat Lux,' primal darkness shimmered into the first day and Earth took form from seething chaos.[33]

Here, the Devil, from the beginning of the conversation, communicates his vital envy, stemming from his inability to create original forms. His pride proves his limits and his end.

The pessimist, who appears more in the mode of a realist, is treated to Lucifer's overarching strategy, which, the Devil exclaims, depends heavily on modern man's belief in the sufficiency of Enlightenment reason and its rejection of original sin to usher in a more fulfilling, beneficent world. The Devil informs him that it was not until he went "underground" that he achieved success unimagined in previous civilizations. Finding the Devil's numerous tales of destruction and death quixotic, the pessimist asks why he insists on an ever-continuing pursuit of annihilation. The Devil says that, arising out of his inability to love, his envy leads only to one course of action: "I possess the will to create (hence my pride), but I am incapable of creating (hence my envy). . . . My greatest masterpiece is never more than a perversion."[34] These lines suggest that Chambers's own view of evil is classical in its formulation: evil is an all-consuming force, but one that remains derivative of the fundamental goodness of being.

The Devil's quest to eliminate man, and the various stratagems and manifestations it takes—total wars, atomic weaponry, death camps, and political revolutions—emerges from his disgust that he cannot create and diffuse goodness across creation. Man, who is capable of using his exclusive gifts as a rational being to express his notions of truth, however limited and faulty they may be, ultimately becomes the object of the Devil's envy and scorn. Thus his task has always been to thwart, disorient, deceive, and bend the deliberate will of man away from objects of goodness and towards the never-ceasing catastrophes of human judgment. Chambers revesals the peculiar relief of this notion when the Devil states, "And yet it is at this very point that man, the monstrous midget, still has the edge on the Devil: he suffers." Suffering, the Devil explains, is the inexpressible action of man produced by the knowledge that his own creativity, stemming as it does from his goodness and love, will fall silent in his demise. Man, the being of tortured complexities, wishes ultimately to create from the center of his soul, and agonizes the moment this possibility begins to slip from him. The nature of man's limitedness informs Satan's concluding statement that the probabilities for success in annihilating human existence have never been so favorable as they are at the midpoint of the twentieth century.

Chambers displays the limitedness of man and its tragic implications from a different horizon in the essay "Faith for a Lenten Age," which primarily explores Reinhold Niebuhr's reclamation of a realist Christian theology for modern man. The tragic sense issues from the dualistic components of man expressed in terms of his soul and body, his reason and his irrationality, his freedom and his limitedness, all pushing him in directions fundamentally in tension with one another.[35] Man fully experiences himself in his ceaseless attempts to mount above his finitude, but with the frightening knowledge of his soul and its powers of rationality and freedom. Man, however, understands deeply the twinned components of being, his freedom and finitude, chiefly through his anxiety, which is responsible for both sin and creativity.[36] Anxiety is the perpetual driver of human experience that frequently leads man awry; a state never more easily reached than in the age of reason. Haunted by his own mortality, anxiety represents that feature of experience where man wrestles with the prospect of his own worth and attempts through labor, thought, and prayer to mount above his flickering life.

The anxiety of man is also the everlasting taint on human action, even in man's creations and advances.[37] Anxiety's compelling nature is its inexorable strain that leads man to sin in mistaken and disturbed attempts either to run from his freedom and sink "in some aspect of the world's vitalities" or to overcome his finitude by "asserting his power beyond the limits of his nature."[38] The latter is emblematic of modernist ideological terror, which in this view remains a near-constant element of human life. However, in an era that has eclipsed the sovereignty of God and transferred a total self-sovereignty to the individual, man moves beyond the limits of his nature and his humanity with frightening regularity. Chambers believed the dissolution of the paradox between man's freedom and his limits was "the sin of the 20th Century."[39] Thus, man's anxiety—the consequence of his paradoxical being—leads to sin and folly, and yet even in his glory man cannot outstrip its shadow, according to Chambers. Man's history is crooked for "even moral achievement of sin is not so easy to purge as moralists imagine."[40]

Interwoven in Chambers's distillation of Niebuhr's account of the human person is Dostoevsky's theological brief that man does not have the answer for evil, a reality never more apparent than when he attempts to deny his end in God. Man's elastic capacity to produce misery is fully realized when he attempts to resolve existential anxiety by severing himself from God. Sin, however, is not the inevitable conclusion of anxiety; there remains the fruit of faith which can release man from such results. Moreover, as Niebuhr explained, sin has entered into the tragedy of existence through an external source; Adam's sin was not the first sin. Yet man remains under its presence, always stumbling, even in his moments of glory.[41]

Emerging from Chambers's rejection of the optimism and thin rationality of the modern liberal project is the obverse of the despair that has to come to characterize the unreflective, postmodern rejection of this same tradition of thought. Convinced of the equal untruth and worthlessness of man's prior and contemporary attempts to understand the grounding of his being and of his purposes, the postmodern mind is unable to consider Chambers's conclusions. Apparent in Chambers's writings is that man's tragic sense and destiny are comprehensible, even elevating, when embraced as a sign toward a higher end. If man's anxiety began with the question "What is Man?" then the answer, Chambers said, begins in the knowledge of an end and purpose higher than man—an end and purpose that draws man upwards, directs his wandering wonder, and perfects his incompleteness.

The Meaning of Conversion

Chambers's personal conversion exemplified the macro-phenomenon he prescribed for Western civilization as a whole. In his moment of *kénosis,* Chambers argued that Communism, at one with the modern mind, was rejected for a world under God. But Chambers made clear that converting to Christianity and jettisoning Communism were not enough. It would be pointless to reject Communism as a political force, but not the modern mind of Enlightenment rationalism. For one still "denies the soul in the name of the mind, and the soul's salvation here and now."[42] For Chambers, Enlightenment rationalism was the authentic source of modernist ideology and its parade of death: the world remained the ultimate stage of human action upon which ideology annihilated ideology. Deformed conscience and its perverse actions were the indispensable partners in butchery, for "the gas ovens of Buchenwald and the Communist execution cellars exist first within our minds."[43]

The central meaning and lasting import of *Witness* is located in these conversion passages. Here Chambers eloquently detailed the immense movement of heart and soul he had undergone. Resembling St. Augustine's *Confessions* and *City of God*, *Witness* communicates Chambers's conversion in a manner that transcends ideology, providing the primal outline of renewal to the West. Moreover, like St. Augustine defending an infant Christianity against accusations of complicity in Rome's destruction, Chambers makes his stand against the overweening rationalism of modern Western thought and the aspersions it casts on Christian insight. As discussed in the previous chapter, Communism never stood alone. Its form and shape were molded, in Chambers's rendition, by basic errors of thought in the Enlightenment.

Chambers looked to medieval Christianity and the Protestant Reformation for insights into man's being—insights that the modern mind had erroneously buried.[44] To understand the exemplary content Chambers intended for his conversion one must look to his admonitions to the West that overcoming Communism could happen only through suffering and the consequent recovery of its vital spiritual content. Chambers, the counterrevolutionary, communicated through his own dark night of the soul that the West, too, could have such hope if it would undergo a similar period of mortification. In recalling these truths the West would rise as the victor, because it would again understand the measure and object of its existence.

The comparison of a civilization-wide turning and Chambers's personal metamorphosis can be observed in the unfolding of events and realizations in his personal narrative. These, in turn, spawn still greater insights into the nature of his actions and their meaning for the West. Chambers provides the shape of this retrieval and rally for the West in his passages on *kénosis*. He reports that as a man of the twentieth century, he plunged into Communism, not as a result of Marxist economics, or the Marxist dialectic and the surety of the Communist project, but from a belief that it answered the modern world's gaping crises.[45] Chambers fully subscribed to the ideology: "It demanded of me those things which have always stirred what is best in men—courage, poverty, self-sacrifice, discipline, intelligence, my life, and, at need, my death."[46] New life and new hope were the chief offerings of Communist revolution. As Chambers elsewhere describes, there was now "A reason to live, and a reason to die."[47]

Telling in this regard was Lenin's pamphlet "A Soviet at Work," which Chambers recalled reading as a Columbia student. The pamphlet detailed a heroic life of daily sacrifice.[48] None of the other writings Chambers encountered in his leftist program of study offered the spirit of Lenin's pamphlet, which exhibited something imperative to Chambers: "The reek of life was on it."

. . . I faced the necessity to act."[49] Like many intellectuals of his period, Chambers was entranced by a Communist program that proclaimed the unqualified solution to the crises of the early twentieth century. Chambers, however, differed from many of this ilk, not merely in leaving Communism but also in rejecting its entire philosophical structure. This was Chambers's distinguishing characteristic: he joined Communism without reservation, accepting a role in the Communist underground when asked, even at the cost of his towering writing career, only to retract everything when Communism's evil brushed against him.

After separating himself from Communism, and equally from Enlightenment rationalism and humanism, Chambers turned toward the West and held out this same promise of conversion and renewal. The project pursued by Chambers was to root liberalism differently than had been done by the broad thrusts of modernist thought. Rather than placing an excarnated mind at the center of existence, as modernist thought had done, Chambers located man in his full bodily and spiritual reality and articulated a humane order from a premodern anthropology. Man's freedom, hence his dignity, was not founded on his autonomous ability to project control through the pursuit of an abstractly conceived perfection. The structure of reality, and the *conditio humana* within it, urges one to the service of transcendence. Man's being was better realized through this recognition of an ordered reality that he, in part, constituted.

Chambers's own course had been mined with frequent peril and material deprivations had been severe. In between his run from the Communist underground and his first subsequent remunerative work, Chambers and his wife went without regular meals for the benefit of their children. Chambers, though, told of still greater harms when describing his turning. Passages like the following from *Witness* give further insight into his suffering: "So great an effort, quite apart from its physical and practical hazards, cannot occur without a profound upheaval of the spirit. No man lightly reverses the faith of an adult lifetime, held implacably to the point of criminality."[50] Further, Chambers notes, "It is not a matter of leaving one house and occupying another" when the caretaker of the second house is "largely witless."[51] There were no hosannas for those who left Communism. For many who had deserted ideological faith there was only a cavern of soul with no other ideals, principles, or faiths capable of answering the freshly encountered existential questions of the ex-Communist.

Heavy in Chambers's thoughts during the winter of 1937—the interlude between his complex realization of Communism's dark logic and his exodus from it—was John Milton's *Samson Agonistes,* a retelling of the Bible's story of Samson.[52] Chambers quotes Samson's opening lines to great effect in *Witness:*

> Promise was that I
> Should Israel from Philistian yoke deliver.
> Ask for this great deliverer now, and find him
> Eyeless in Gaza, at the mill with slaves.[53]

This citation further reinforces Chambers's understanding of personal conversion and its salutary cultural and civilizational consequences. Once believing that he possessed the strength to liberate a captive Western humanity through Communist ideology,

Chambers now realized that he, too, was a slave toiling mindlessly at the mill. The larger implication is that Chambers, like Samson, will break his bonds and bring down the house of his enemy, even to the point of destroying himself.[54] Similar to Samson's decision to actuate his divine appointment, Chambers will translate his graced being into an instrument of American redemption.

This redemption brings to one's full attention the moral meaning of the Hiss case, which provided the compelling rationale for Chambers's decision to become an informant in 1948. Like Samson, whose strength returned and brought down the Philistines, Chambers courageously ended the false grandeur of Alger Hiss. Such courage sprang from the depths of his rejection of Communism, entangled as it was, in this particular instance, with his attempt to bring Hiss out of Communism with him.[55] Hiss had not obliged, and agreed with his wife, during that fateful conversation, that Chambers's exhortations to leave Communism were an exercise in "mental masturbation."[56] The bare fact in Chambers's conscience was that men of talent and access to power had aligned themselves with Stalin—that is, they had been complicit in the central workings of evil which now threatened America. The reference to Samson now becomes complete, for as the biblical character achieves his divinely appointed task only through his death, Chambers brings justice to Hiss's treachery and ends his prominence only through losing his reputation, security, and livelihood.[57]

Informing Chambers's decision to testify before the House Committee on Un-American Activities was the matter of his personal responsibility, heightened, he believed, by the notion that "with each passing year, the free world shrank in power and faith, including faith in itself, and sank deeper into intellectual and moral chaos."[58] Regarding the rejuvenation of the intellectual and spiritual resources of the West, Chambers offered another understanding of the existential decisions made by his fellow moderns. These choices Chambers proclaimed as the life of the political revolutionary and the life of bourgeois success.[59] Stating that he had lived both poles of existence and was currently embarked, as a senior editor of *Time*, on the life of success, Chambers stepped forward to provide a third existence, which he achieved as witness and informant.

With his actual witness, Chambers demanded that the observer understand that both narratives—a life of revolution and life of success—are incapable of fulfilling man's essential nature. The former perversely attempted it, but ended in the elimination of man. The latter gave man previously unimagined levels of comfort, choice, and material development, but, taken alone, it proved inadequate to the exceptionalism of man, marked as he is by spirit and reason. The narrative that Chambers attempted to impress upon America was both "religious and moral." The experiences marked by components of religion and morality were the only ones capable of giving "men the heart to suffer the ordeal of a life that perpetually rends them between its beauty and its terror."[60] A new ending for man was required. Sacrifice and courage were necessary in the effort to uphold America's sacred political and spiritual principles. The principles that had been questioned and found wanting by certain members of the nation's governing elite would have to be vindicated, again.

The mass savagery conducted by totalitarian regimes expressed the further meaning, Chambers believed, of a broken humanity.

Under systematic state-enforced violence entire sections of people within states had fallen victims to terror. These crimes could not be easily cabined or buried in man's conscience. Chambers expressed that man and community were a whole; deprivations and loss imposed on one section of humanity remained latent in man's conscience requiring atonement. Otherwise, their dead bodies remained unburied. As in the Katyn Forest massacre, or the bureaucratized slaughter at the Hotel Lux, explanations and rationalizations from secular reason were inconclusive for such ends. Or as he explained to William F. Buckley Jr.:

> The age is impaled on its most maiming experience, namely, that a man can be . . . wiped out, regardless of what he is, means, hopes, dreams or might become. This reality cuts across our minds like a wound whose edges crave to heal, but cannot. Thus, one of the great sins, perhaps *the* great sin, is to say: It will heal; it has healed; there is no wound; there is something more important than this wound. There is nothing more important than this wound. If we cannot learn to get beyond it, to find meaning which includes it, the age can solve nothing for itself.[61]

Chambers added, "It is forbidden us to turn away from the wound. You perhaps do not remember the mass graves of the First World War in Poland. But you do remember the Katyn Forest. It is not just those bodies that lie heaped there. It is that we lie, smothering alive, under the heaps."[62]

In short, Chambers insisted that the fallen victims of the ideological age will have to be accounted for in manners and means beyond government statistics, reparations commissions, and national memorials. Their lives—consumed by man's primordial thirst to organize himself without God, even against God, which was made manifest in the most voracious of ways in totalitarian ideology—would need God to be vindicated.

Chambers's commitment to offer himself as a sacrifice in redemption of the West's truths led him to take action as informant. The beginning of the repair of the breach of goodness and unity within the modern West could be had at no lesser price.

CHAPTER FOUR

THE CONSERVATIVE SPIRIT

THIS INVESTIGATION INTO THE THOUGHT of Whittaker Chambers focuses on the spiritual and existential treatment he offered to the overarching malaise of the West in the twentieth century. However, it is a disservice to Chambers to bypass the fragments of meaning in his writing, which, when collected, approach a political remedy for the "open wound" produced by modern ideology. While Chambers never viewed the political order as a determinant of man's measure, he did contemplate the need for a politics that could account for the fullness of man's lived experiences in the era of late modernity. Given his express denial of an inner eschatological capability to politics Chambers articulated a political theory that permitted the enduring truths of man's experiences to shape a restrained political order.

In this vein Chambers listed a series of principles, concerns, and hopes he believed necessary to any conservative movement in order to successfully challenge the regnant orthodoxy of Leftist thought. The proper objects of conservatism were succinctly disclosed by Chambers to William F. Buckley Jr. in the following statement:

"The conservative position defends and invokes those great truths which the mind of the West has once for all disclosed."[1] Truth, then, becomes the watchword for conservatism. Conservatism's vindication emerged through expressing the nature of man's being and its requirements for a life well lived.

Chambers gave solicitous regard to an animating center of ideas that would vitally inform modern conservatism with definitive content from which the "conservative spirit" could propel itself to victory, intellectually and politically. This quest was towards something everlasting in the political and social order. As Chambers stated in his last piece of correspondence with Buckley, "each age finds its own language for an eternal meaning." Chambers's attempt to find habits of being in cultures and civilizations that express man's recurrent hopes and practices, as seen in the ordering of his work, family, and political life, was evident. Moreover, openness to the divine ground of being was pivotal to Chambers's search. For Chambers, the conservative position needed to mount higher than the conservative individualism of Frank S. Meyer and similar writers of the period. Additionally, appeals made by others to tradition or a traditionalist aesthetic were incomplete because they could not account for the full complexities and paradoxes of the modern democratic situation. Uneasy with being called a conservative, Chambers referred to himself as a "Man of the Right." However, his actual writing on this subject and its emanating style, not to mention the force of his life, portray Chambers more as a counterrevolutionary. Chambers's focus was to recover and assert the supreme philosophical and cultural truths that would finally dislodge the Leftist juggernaut.[2]

Chambers the counterrevolutionary, however, presents a series of challenges in reconciling the disparate elements of thought evident in his own mind and life. While declaiming against the specific label of conservatism, his writing manifested the enduring elements of liberty, authority, property, spirit, and tradition that have always formed the substance of this body of thought in America. The particular quandary for contemporary conservatism, Chambers believed, was the parochialism of its objects and its consequent inability to draw clear, coherent skirmish lines with Leftism. Thus, this inability to adequately understand its own core principles underserved the Right in its debate with collectivism.

Further tensions seem to emerge when Chambers's counterrevolutionary pronouncements are compared with his forceful statements and reasoning against Enlightenment rationalism. Chambers's statements against this mode of thought evince his disdain for the radical and exclusivist role it demands of politics. His understanding of the human person, best observed in the essay "Faith for a Lenten Age," contributes to a moderate and restrained posture for politics given man's irresolvable tensions. Yet the counterrevolutionary position, which necessarily issues into direct action against a settled body of doctrine and thought, must assume at a certain level the very political posture Chambers decries. That is, one must be willing to overturn practices, habits, and traditions of an opposing ideology if one is to find success as a counterrevolutionary. The rawer aspects of politics are affirmed, unfortunately.

The tension inherent in these two approaches of Chambers as a counterrevolutionary and his understanding of the inherent limitations of politics is never fully resolved in Chambers's thought. His writing, however, also implicates what the German political theorist Carl Schmidt termed "the age of the exception." Thus, Chambers's counterrevolutionary position becomes justified under the dispensation of the exceptional interval of history he lived in. This moment demanded a certain political bellicosity to halt the advance of Communism, both at home and abroad. Chambers's generation needed to locate itself and give its witness of an eternal meaning through an intellectual and political program that positively denied the throne to the devotees of socialism.

Although Chambers intended to detail a conservative program, unfortunately he did not leave behind any well-laid theory in this regard. Mastering the present through meditatively re-collecting the past, made possible by correct orientation to reality was foremost in Chambers's writing. He placed less hope in the fusionism of free markets and bourgeois virtues that defined the broad consensus of conservative writing in the postwar decades. Chambers held no brief for conservatism finding its redemptive sword in an all-encompassing embrace of rational autonomy issuing from a primarily negative account of man's orientation to truth. Chambers never rejected these arguments outright, but he judged them as deficient in meeting the more enduring needs of contemporary man.[3]

Interestingly, Chambers pointed towards the oldest spiritual institution in the West—the Roman Catholic Church—as the organ closest to his ideal of a counterrevolutionary spirit. On this front, Chambers's judgment was unequivocal:

There is only one fully logical conservative position in the West—that of the Catholic Church. It has nothing to do with Frank Chodorov. But I think it has a good deal to do with Frank Meyer. Otherwise there are only schism and heresy. Moreover, the Church is the only true counterrevolutionary force, not because it contains the political revolution in this world, but because it contains the revolution wherever the revolution manifests the wound.[4]

Chambers's mention of Frank Chodorov and Frank Meyer brings to relief his larger point of the Church's ancient wisdom and contemporary political difficulties. Chodorov, an anarchist important postwar commentator on market economics, was a signature figure in early movement conservatism, but one who largely rejected the attempt to salvage the foundational moral and religious heritage of the West in modern politics. Less dismissive of this approach was Frank Meyer, but Chambers suggests his individualism left little space for a significant contribution from the reserves of mercy and reflective habits of the premodern period. The focus of Chambers's judgment, here, was the Roman Church's position as a bedrock of truth from which the modern might regain his orientation—understanding his nature through spiritual and philosophical meditation. The inherent failure in foregoing this tradition of insight and wisdom was in man being reduced to something less than who he is: "This age is of a grandeur that it sins against persistently by not letting itself know. Each of us, Frank too, must beware of letting ourselves be less than what is."[5]

The intellectual and moral freefall that Chambers believed

was the essence of modern thought was staved off by a church that did not deny the "wound" of contemporary existence, but instead sought to make perennial realities intelligible once again. As noted in the previous chapter, Chambers's understanding of this wound was not entirely bound up with the ravages of modern ideology, but incorporated all of human error and folly, "where the spear, century by century, pierces the side."[6] Original sin is the wound that Chambers refers to in this selection. Its heaviness consists in the constant temptations, crimes, and miseries of man that perpetually distort his efforts. Man's peculiar predicament, however, had become acute in an era when the moral law itself was not only disobeyed but was not even formally acknowledged. Only the Roman Catholic Church, Chambers argued, had the spiritual and intellectual resources to stare at the "torrent, and measure what it costs a man's soul to make its passage." The passage was for the man of late modernity to again recover himself from the vast gulf of dislocation and suffering imposed by the total wars and state-inflicted homicides of the twentieth century. Even in the democratic populations of the West Chambers found the abandonment of the possibilities of transcendent meaning and purpose. Similarly, Chambers saw the banality of democracy when it no longer was informed by conscience and moral responsibility for those certain goods that transcended man's experiences.

The conservative spirit found apt expression in Chambers's correspondence with Ralph de Toledano, where Chambers observed its emanation throughout the centuries "in chains of succession and authority."[7] Conservatism became the recognition of what is consubstantial to man's existence carried, as it were, *à la fine pointe de l'âme* (at the forefront of the soul).[8] In Chambers's rendering, conservatism existed beyond the level of authority and mere tradition, or, rather, it came to assume authority and tradition because it recognized the common graces of life and enjoined them to man's understanding.

Intelligible to conservatism, this chain of grace bound men to it in an authentic manner with power beyond that of force and authority. Thus, modern ideologies that attempted to create new forms of spirit by which man overcame his given alienation inherently failed. In imprisoning reality through iron laws of history by which mental and social constructs interpreted man's being to himself there came to be only force and authority. Man became the servant and instrument of power expressed by the modern ideological state. Conservatism's common grace was its rejection of the abstract vise-grip employed by the various "-isms" that sought to encapsulate man in a worldy existence. In this manner, conservatism for Chambers was simply the proper recognition of man as a rational being capable of apprehending meaning beyond the sensible, laboring through both thought and spiritual capacities to higher realities.

The Sources of Renewal

Chambers's sense that conservatism must point towards higher, everlasting ideas about man becomes more evident in the essays he penned for *Life*'s "History of Western Culture" series. Spanning from the demise of the Roman Empire through the close of Victorian England and the onset of the Great War, Chambers focused on the intractable dimensions of Western man in each age. The figures explored by Chambers in these essays continually confront their longings for God, fellow man, political order, commerce, and geographical and artistic exploration. The theme guiding these essays is the object of man's loves, and what he worships, and how these things reveal each age with exceptional clarity. Two essays, "The Sanity of St. Benedict" and "The Protestant Revolution," particularly embody this strain of Chambers's thought.

Earnestly laboring under the belief that the West was likely to be swallowed by Communism and its related perversities, Chambers looked to the periods in Western history when other political, cultural, and social dissolutions had occurred. Here one sees distinctive aspects of Chambers's conservatism. For Chambers the sources of renewal could be found in the fateful steps taken by individuals in the aftermaths of prior collapses in the West.

Present in these investigations is an assessment comparable to a Voegelinian understanding of political, social, and cultural order whereby authority is understood as comprising three elements: power, reason, and revelation.[9] Authority is a natural aspect of shared humane existence that is founded and understood through a process of metaphysical reasoning. Additionally, the component of revelation provides a higher authority, and is inherent in man's need to understand the basis of being.

In the collapse of earlier periods of high civilization Chambers saw the accompanied diminishment of belief in the purpose of the civilization itself by its citizens. The collective purpose of the varied elements within the civilization no longer commanded the love and the creative faculties of the people comprising it. Dismissing material, political, and economic explanations as comprehensive rationales for the Roman Empire's collapse, Chambers found the rise of the Benedictine Order at the Empire's end as the unique, paradoxical sign of exhaustion in Roman civilization.[10]

Located southeast of Rome in Monte Cassino, the beginning of this small monastic community became, in time, the curious bearer of a new order arising from the fading empire. Regarding the redemptive capacity of the Benedictine Rule Chambers asserted:

> For those who obeyed it, it ended three great alienations of the spirit whose action, I suspect, touched on that missing something which my instructors failed to find among the causes of the fall of Rome. The same alienations, I further suspect, can be seen at their work of dissolution among ourselves, and are perhaps among the little noticed reasons why men turn to Communism. They are: the alienation of the spirit of man from traditional authority; his alienation from the idea of traditional order; and a crippling alienation that he feels at the point where civilization has deprived him of the joy of simple productive labor.[11]

Chambers the counterrevolutionary, whose primary concern was for the West to again speak to the truth of man's being, located the effusive stream of Benedictine community as an acute cultural instance to which the modern imagination might look for understanding. Moreover, the cultural shift inherent in the rise of Benedict's order led Chambers to question the dominance of the Whig theory of history, which posited that the Anglo-Saxon political tradition consisted in the ever-broadening circle of liberty and civil order flowing from the expansion of reason and rights in the modern period. Benedict's attempt at renewal, Chambers suggested, offered the better path to the truly liberal order because it was premised on the unique design of the human person—its sacred and profane tendencies.

Benedict, among others, was to be the cultural heir of the fallen Western portion of Roman civilization. Chambers viewed Benedict's success as that of a creative steward who built on "traditional authority," "simple labor," and the worship of God. Benedict's burden was to re-collect portions of Rome's broken glory and join it to a new rush of spirit that would carry Classical, Roman, and Christian civilization forward amidst the falling night. As Chambers stated:

> At the touch of his mild inspiration, the bones of a new order stirred and clothed themselves with life; drawing to itself much of what was best and most vigorous among the ruins of man and his work in the Dark Ages, and conserving and shaping its energy for that unparalleled outburst of mind and spirit in the Middle Ages.

Benedict's shoring up of the fragments of civilization and forming them with grace represented for Chambers the authentic process of renewal. The false choice exercised by the modern West existed in the illusion that man could abstractly impose order in all areas of life. This illusion emerged from insisting upon the primacy of an element of man's existence—security, property, or individuality depending upon which philosopher was talking—and through an ever-extending process of rationality making it the nucleus of the social order. Benedict's order takes man concretely, joining his natural desires for community, labor, and authority under a divine dispensation. Chambers's quest for the deposit of goodness to which the conservatism of his era must appeal, and from which it must learn, finds expression in Benedict's inspired establishment of a new, humane order.[12]

The onset of a genuine Dark Ages, from Chambers's perspective, was best viewed as the sequestration of man from his authentic, natural tendencies and longings in favor of an artificial order constructed on an abstraction of man from his complete person. Thus, Enlightenment *philosophes* erred in their judgment that the period between the fall of Rome and the rise of Renaissance Humanism was a period of rank illiberalism. Such an assessment revealed more about the Enlightenment's liberationist conceit of autonomous reason than the intellectual and cultural deficiencies of the premodern West. Chambers noted ironically at the essay's end of a new Dark Ages that had fallen paradoxically on the parts of Europe ruled by Communism, the most logical intellectual summation of the Age of Reason. The task that again fell on Western man, if he was to preserve civilization, was the benevolent work of Benedict.

Continuing in this historical vein Chambers's essay "The Middle Ages" looked at a civilization in which man's supreme craving for "Light" was acknowledged and carried throughout his life, instantiated in his community, labor, and thought.[13] The alienation of man from God that characterized much of modern thought was meritless in this order of ideas. If all things were possible to science according to the modern man, the medieval man knew better: all things were possible to faith, its power revealed in the path to God it provided. Moreover, the unifying vision of the age contained and enforced its humane order; "the sweetness of the medieval mind" emerged from the charity revealed to man by God. In knowing the divine ground of one's being and the source of its order one experiences the love that demands, in turn, its own greater response.

The enduring order, according to Chambers, found expression in another source of conservatism: early modern Protestant theology. Exemplified in his essay "The Protestant Revolution," Chambers offered the example of a Welsh Protestant martyr as revelatory of the greater cultural truth of belief and witness.[14] Again, as in prior essays on Benedict and the medieval period, Chambers paid high regard to the religious-cultural forms that infused life and summoned forth praise and obedience from men. Directly aware of man's peculiar longing to believe in and to love God, guided as this is by man's obsession with his own limitedness and mortality, Chambers emphasized that such loves and obsessions are a permanent feature of man's being. They are also inevitably reflected in the social and political order consequent to the cultural order becoming integrated with the contents of these central goods.

Chambers's use of the fisherman-martyr, Rawlins White, in the essay was related to his understanding of conservatism. Recalling Chambers's notion that the West must suffer to realize its former greatness and defeat Communism, the martyr becomes the witness whose exemplary teaching goes forward beyond his death. Undeterred by final offers of repentance from Catholic clergy, Rawlins White bore his Protestant theological conviction until its last bitter dregs were consumed. Chambers wrote, "For few, whatever their beliefs, could fail to sense that when a fisherman, as obscure as any who fished in Galilee, chose to die in fire rather than deny his faith, there was at work in the world a force capable of transforming it."[15] Demonstrated in martyrdom, forged in the ghastly horror of men committing other men to death, are the existential commitments of the age.

These commitments proclaim their rising power over souls, seeking to displace the prevailing order no longer able to compel similar sacrifices. As Chambers insisted, "martyrdoms . . . are never solutions but pyres whose flicker is addressed, not primarily to the present, but to a posterity that has not yet cohered out of chaos and old night."[16] Thus, the able quality of Chambers's counterrevolutionary conservatism is now thrown into high relief. The search becomes one not just for a humane order, but for the methods and teaching moments that make it realizable in the modern age.

Chambers held that his testimony against Hiss was a witness in the complete sense: affirming truth against its corruption, even to the point of total ruin. Such a witness was repeatedly discussed by Chambers throughout his writing career, from the Bolshevik short stories penned for *The New Masses,* to "The Protestant Revolution," to his searing meditations on the meaning of his own witness and its portent for American conservatism. In letters penned to Buckley that describe his counterrevolutionary conservatism, Chambers, at one point, appealed to the Narodniki, the anarchic socialists of pre-Leninist Russia, describing them as "those who went with bomb or revolver against this or that individual monster," to emphasize the form of both his commitment to Communism and his later denouncement of the ideology.[17] The Narodniki's "revolutionary spirit blends with a Christian élan," lending its ideological character to the substantive spirituality necessary for its sacrifices.

Chambers held that such spirit remained extant in the Fourth Section of Soviet Military Intelligence (Chambers's section) years after its official extermination during the Stalinist purges.[18] Moreover, Chambers pointed to Saranov—the Narodniki member who, in protest of prison conditions, lit himself aflame in a Tsarist prison camp—as his inspiration for the particular courage to inform against Hiss.[19] Elsewhere, Chambers recalled Joan of Arc. Her witness was the "effective assertion" that "not words, but the play of fire seals man's hope and faith that there is a reality beyond and above the merely worldly reality of the turning wheel of history."[20] Joan of Arc, like Saranov, was fully conscious of her mind, and, in giving her life, she reflected her "hold of a deeper reality" and the need for higher order.

The Everlasting Quality

On a practical level, the need for definite conservative principles arose because most of the rising claimants to this mantle were unable to speak authoritatively. Chambers observed, "The heart of the great problem is, what makes the Conservative position so unappealing? What makes this great central position of mankind so much a skeleton of dried bones? Why to put it simply, has the right scarcely a voice that speaks for it with authority or conviction— or without the curse of faint apology?"[21] Chambers's criticism of Russell Kirk's *The Conservative Mind* speaks against the circuitous approaches to a definite Rightist program taken by many conservative authors in the twentieth century. Kirk's ambitious attempt to articulate an aesthetic, almost Platonic conservatism in a line of thinkers from Edmund Burke to T. S. Eliot drew applause from Chambers, but it failed to pass his test of clear principle and a program for action.[22] Where Kirk recovered traditionalist thought, rediscovering the concept of "moral imagination"—a way of applying right reason to modern disorder—Chambers desired a program of intellectual force, capable of direct application against the Left. Chambers stated, "Informed the book is; worthy it is—a worthy master's thesis. And, *faute de mieux* [for lack of anything better], we do well to push it. But if you were a marine in a landing boat, would you wade up the seabeach at Tarawa for that conservative position? And neither would I!"[23]

Forcing the deathworks of socialism and its false narrative of human flourishing remained the pivotal moment for any conservatism that was to shape the current scene, Chambers held. Not only would it have to carry the burden of argument, it had to break through the encrustation of recent orthodoxy, which had smothered the spirit that conservatism must locate and proclaim. The everlasting quality of the conservative spirit was the predicate to an effective counterrevolutionary program. Chambers's idea of the essence of conservatism was Aristotelian. Political truths were not philosophical forms brought down into the city but emerged through experience and subsequent reflection:

Ages change, politics shift and slither—the conservative spirit does not change. It adjusts—because it is the summation of human wisdom, and in a sense organic, it looks from the fastness of life, and bends or yields to what is passing, but maintains, as the light shines in darkness, what is everlasting because it partakes of it itself.[24]

Chambers hoped that in going beyond the conservative position to the conservative spirit something affirmative and rejuvenating could happen in Western political life.[25] Chambers thought uncovering this spirit was crucial, for its beauty rested in its truth, and in its truth was the motivating moment of action, seen when the principle stirred both military draftee and businessman.

Yet Chambers's arguments for an acclimatized conservatism are surprising given his Manichean reading of the Cold War and the crisis of the West. The insights rendered by Chambers in his correspondence with Buckley seem at odds with the Chambers of *Witness*. In his autobiography Chambers, unlike many political observers, refuses to theoretically separate the strands of Leftist political thought. For Chambers, there is only, in Voegelin's memorable phrase, the constant attempt by the Left "to immanentize the eschaton." The response to this basic thrust of the Left, proclaimed Chambers, was for men of conscience, patriotism, and faith to rally against all aspects of its underlying project of political redemption. Chambers does not consider prudence in this political and intellectual counter-assault, allowing for many to see in *Witness* an un-American intolerance that is ill-suited for politics in a democracy. In this view of Chambers, the only voices that he can finally hear are the cries of extreme human action.

Clearly, Chambers had adjusted his own thinking on the steps needed to salvage the American regime. The observation that conservatism "adjusts—because it is the summation of human wisdom" demands one's attention, because Chambers looked for an affirmative base that could advance the "organic" cultural-political ideals of the West in "the fastness of life."[26] Inherent in Chambers's analysis was the knowledge that anti-Communism alone could not provide the spirit or intellect to any counterrevolutionary movement that would re-occupy terrain formerly conceded to the Left.

Chambers's insistence on positive content for any political movement that would effectively countermand the Left was characteristic of his meditations on "the total crisis" and the pedagogical meaning of suffering for a degenerating West. Politics and its composite parts of polemics and political theorizing were spiritual and moral enterprises for Chambers. Their purpose was to help man understand certain truths about himself and his responsibilities, enabling him to choose the best purposes and objects for his actions individually and collectively in the polity.

For Chambers, the principled position was not one of utilitarian calculation or a means to merely sharpen one's arguments against an ideological foe. Certainly, the intrinsic merit of the principled position was its act of definition. Even more, though, for Chambers, the resultant clarity enabled one to pursue political objects in concert with others fully aware of the movement's standards of judgment and strategic goals.[27] Moreover, careful definition of the position produced the corollary flexibility in tactics necessary for any political movement to achieve success in modern democratic societies.[28] Such elasticity in tactics formed a sure part of Chambers's "conservative spirit," as he explained in his letters to Buckley.

Chambers imparted the agility and prudence of his counter-revolutionary conservatism in exchanges with Buckley and Willi Schlamm. The correspondence was driven by Buckley's desire to found *National Review* and his related desire for Chambers to be an editor of the journal. Chambers related the direction such a publication must take American conservatism if it were to make the movement a success. Chambers's point of view did not easily cohere with the conservative, fusionist animus of Buckley and Schlamm, and later, Frank Meyer. Greatly concerned with the political quali-ties and tactics that would be shared among the editors, Chambers stated to Buckley, "Your magazine is above all, a moral apologetic; and it had better be good. For a morality is never stronger than the reality it speaks for."[29] Indicative was Chambers's idea that the journal must "win a war rather than defend a position."[30]

Chambers's insistence on strategic advancement against the political Left emerged dramatically in his initial refusal to join *National Review* as an editor. Buckley noted that Chambers's refusal was rooted in his unwillingness to contribute to a publication whose editors held doubts privately, and perhaps publicly, regarding Richard Nixon's future candidacy for the presidency. Chambers feared the consequences of an editorial rejection of Nixon during his presidential campaign. More at stake was the possible jettison-ing of a realist political logic, one that Nixon shared, and which Chambers held as crucial to postwar conservatism.

The logic was that of a clear, yet practical, definition of pur-poses and enemies, coupled with vigorous activity to accumulate intellectual and practical resources. Nixon accomplished this marshalling of forces with masterful effect in the Hiss hearings.

Nixon had ably led the hearings by carrying reluctant committee members over several moments of intense public doubt regarding Chambers's accusations. This leadership, which permitted the hearings to continue, ensured that Chambers's testimony would receive full consideration. At a potential mortal cost to his career, Nixon pursued the strategies of delay and rapid advance, accumulating information against Hiss until the evident problems in his defense proved unavoidable, and then demanded a federal grand jury.

Nixon, through extensive study, had engaged in a fervid, monk-like approach to the hearings, familiarizing himself with the factual material and the personalities of Hiss and Chambers.[31] Nixon also had grasped the validity of Chambers's testimony at a time when many doubted him.[32] Pouncing at a moment of supreme advantage, when Hiss proved to lack credibility before the committee on his central denials of Chambers's testimony, Nixon exploited the hearings for maximum advantage for both himself and for the Republican Party.

By relying on the corroboration of events, facts, and personalities, Nixon utilized the case to generate impressive political capital, vindicating himself as a prophetic Red-hunter. Later, however, Nixon withdrew his anti-Communism from the scene when the situation no longer supported direct action. Nixon's ability to maneuver and operate within the quicksand of media-age politics was frequently unappreciated by many would-be supporters. However, such was the language and practice of realist politics: adjustments and maneuvers could produce small but significant victories when aggregated.

In Chambers's view, *National Review* overlooked the task of political practice in a liberal democracy. Buckley and other editors had supported Senator Joseph McCarthy in print and other forums, and, of particular folly to Chambers, had shown a willingness to support a right-wing third party. Chambers believed that the adoption of a third party would start a rapid asphyxiation of successful conservative politics. Prior to the 1956 election when Eisenhower's health seemed a barrier to a second term, Chambers thought a third party's principal effect would only be to negate Vice President Nixon's candidacy, ensuring a Democratic victory. Those who entertained such political projects were, in Chambers's mind, deeply unserious persons, unable to engage the Left prudently. Committed to political purity, coupled with unrealistic goals of repealing early twentieth century federal policy innovations, Chambers found the third-party stance unworthy of his support. [33]

Chambers exemplified the shrewdness of his judgment with his analysis of the painful situation of the Roman Catholic churches in Poland and Hungary under Soviet rule.[34] Cardinal Mindszenty, the leader of the Hungarian church, took the more perilous path of complete resistance to the Soviets, which earned him prison, brief liberation during the resistance of '56, and then confinement to the American embassy for much of the Cold War. The church in Hungary was subjugated and was effectively leaderless for decades owing to Mindszenty's choice to reject any possibility of cooperation with the Soviets.

The leader of Polish Catholics, Cardinal Wyszynski, chose a course of stiff resistance, enduring a brief period in prison, but he also maneuvered the church within and around Soviet dictates. Thus,

Poland saw a moral and spiritual leadership that effectively secured the church into the Communist Polish experience. The possible removal of the church's legitimacy by the Soviets had become incomprehensible because of the cardinal's prudential daring. A choice to severely punish the church would now cost the Soviet dictatorship much international goodwill. Chambers believed that Wyszynski's course preserved the spirit of a nation, enabling it to resist and secure its freedom, as it did, in the appropriate season. Chambers sensed this prophetically in his correspondence with Buckley:

> With the knife at your throat (the situation of the Poles and of their Cardinal), there are only two choices: to maneuver, knowing fully the chances of failure, but remembering that Hope is one of the Virtues; or to hold your neck still to the knife in the name of martyrdom.
>
> But just here is the crux. We are not talking about the Church Triumphant. We are talking about the Church in this world, the world of Warsaw and of Budapest, whose streets are of a drabness that squeezed the blood from the heart. In that sad light, the figure of the Polish Cardinal is a figure of hope.[35]

Of course, Poland, ignited by Pope John Paul II's visit in 1979, the first year of his Pontificate, engaged in broad-scale resistance throughout the 1980s and peacefully earned its freedom. None deny the strength of the Polish Church and the spiritual verve it provided to this effort. Yet as Chambers predicted six months after the failed 1956 Hungarian resistance, the seeds of Polish freedom were planted by the difficult movements made by Wyszynski in the early years of the Soviet imperium.[36] Wyszynski's choice, as Chambers wrote elsewhere, was the strenuous one faced by "the cliff-dancers [who] will hear the screaming curses of those who fall, or be numbed by the sullen silence of those, nobler souls perhaps, who will not join the dance."[37] The Polish cardinal, in leading his own church militant, had held to hope; and in so doing, nourished the only authentic freedom that could speak to men living under the heel of Communist satrapy.

Chambers's realist contention that a successful conservatism must account for the broad trends of modernity was illuminative of his counterrevolutionary strain.[38] Informing this judgment was the acceptance by modern man of Enlightenment rationalism's central ideas and works. Additionally, conservatism had to negotiate the problems created by the significant American departure from certain aspects of the Western tradition.[39] Chambers did not counsel acceptance of the Enlightenment's conceits and works; he understood its long career and the new parameters that now guided Western nations by an advanced secularism, technological dynamism, individualism, capitalism, and the sheer size and intrusiveness of the state.[40] To rally the West, conservatism needed to maneuver within the "interstices" of these factors, which tended to combine and multiply with dizzying rapidity in the cultural, social, political, and economic structures of modern nations.

Curiously, given the wellspring of arguments Chambers made regarding the pitfalls of Leftist *ideology,* he offered a political argument directed primarily against *machines,* and the tremendous adjustments in civilization demanded by technology.[41] Technology had not merely raised living standards but delivered to man the unprecedented possibilities of abundance, ease, equality, as well as the ability to deal death to millions of men in abundance, ease, and equality. The ever-multiplying needs and hopes of the masses, Chambers believed, were themselves the creation of machines.[42] "A conservatism that cannot face the facts of the machine and mass production, and its consequences in government and politics, is foredoomed to futility and petulance. A conservatism that allows for them has an eleventh-hour chance of rallying what is really sound in the West."[43] Chambers, however, was no Luddite, and he proposed that conservatism must incorporate within its moral polemic the substantive implications of advanced mechanized change and development.

Chambers's analysis developed from the enormous innovations wrought within two centuries by science and technological gains to something more, to the consequent social and moral dislocation and confusion. The shocking feature of warfare during the twentieth century, resulting in large part from scientific advances divorced from wisdom, was central to this dislocation. Progress had been separated from the service of the human spirit, according to Chambers. Attempts to arrange these changes within a humane scale had proved largely ineffectual. Chambers's authentic dismay rested in the apathetic failure of a disintegrating West to confront the question of the ends of technology itself, or how a civilized people should incorporate the energy of such discoveries into a moral framework. Conversely, Chambers maintained that the equally errant choice was the simple rejection of such technological discoveries.

Repudiation of scientific and commercial innovation entailed the denial of the new realities of mass modern existence. The import for politics was substantial, as the appetites of the masses, according to Chambers, were continuously shaped by modern technology.[44] However, the dehumanizing possibilities arose from the desires and impulses of the masses who rush forward without the possibility of refined guidance. Progress, as Chambers observed, had been severed from any notion of the good.

This unfortunate reality was chiefly observed in the incessant demands for material abundance and in greater social equality among modern populations, both made more possible by advanced industry and an accommodating democratic state.[45] These demands would inherently produce larger government, as individuals by the principle of representation would seek substantive equality for their awakened passions and desires. From these facts Chambers reached the conclusion that repetitive, conservative paeans to the small government of a past era would only lead to inevitable defeat.

The interests represented by the Republican Party did not stir the same number of "eager voting hands as the Democratic interest."[46] As Chambers stated, "The Republican Party will win the masses, or history will find for it a quiet, uncrowded spot in the potter's field; the grass will grow greenly because no mourning foot will ever tread it down."[47] The real debate, for Chambers, should be in the prudent and wise management of government for humane ends. Proper navigation of the shoals of twentieth century existence required conservatism to proclaim an order of moral coherence. Such consensus would consist of the firm meeting of working-class aspirations with the limited, but necessary, apparatus of government.[48]

Capitalism itself—and the constant disorder introduced to communities and societies by its inevitable works—further animated Chambers's counterrevolutionary conservatism. Not at direct odds with this particular state of affairs, Chambers proclaimed, "I am a man of the Right because I mean to uphold capitalism in its American version."[49] Capitalism's tension with conservatism, however, was immediate and unavoidable, given that its tendencies were towards "perpetual change." The torrential abundance launched by capitalism's unsettling impulses of advance and destruction of both prior industries and social habits garnered Chambers's qualified acceptance, inaugurating, he believed, the vast dimensions of the modern democratic state. Chambers looked to his preferred vocation of farming to explain this dynamic and resisted the much easier turn of blaming capitalism itself.

The new reality of expansionist state policy and the dependency of individuals on its largesse found apt expression in Chambers's series of reflections on "socialist agriculture."[50] With realist dread, Chambers reported the gleaming paradox of his fellow Maryland farmers, who were violently at odds with federal government crop allotment schemes, but simultaneously accepting support checks and various other subsidies. Chambers noted the imbecility of such action for "if you have voted for subsidies, or accepted $ checks, you have also voted for supervision. Who says A must also say B."[51] The Maryland farmers' objections were directed at federal policies that regulated the amount of a specific crop that could be grown even when used only on one's own farm. However, the opposition to federal intervention was not sensible, given their broader acceptance of it when it proved beneficial to their self-interest. Rather, as

Chambers observed, socialism may well be said by future historians to have originated in the countryside.

The farmers' reactions were authentic responses in defense of freedom, Chambers held, particularly the unyielding freedom of choosing the type and quantity of a specific crop to cultivate from the very soil one owned.[52] The larger "impersonal reality" was that the farmers themselves had signed "for a socialist agriculture with their feet." In short, the farmers had remained farmers, content to supply their agricultural labor and operate their farms, even if it was now possible to do so only through federal subsidies and controls. One manifestation of the larger force that confronted the farmers was agricultural technology and its ability to produce yields in greater abundance, at cheaper prices, and with cheaper inputs. Chambers's insight pivoted on the "creative-destructive" aspect of modern capitalism, which, under the democratic principle of representation, operated as an unending invitation to government to manage and smooth its socially agitating tendencies.

The enveloping state, no longer a revolutionary institution, may have become, in the creative-destructive process, the key stabilizing point of modern society. Hence, the modern state performed its own conservative role. Chambers's fellow farmers became increasingly unnecessary given the rapid advancements made in agricultural industry; thus the management of their farms by government was a charitable, yet dangerous, course of action if one's concern was for liberty. The difficulty was in the farmer's acceptance of leaving his land and livelihood under the pressure of modern economies of scale.

Chambers's analysis of the antithesis of capitalism and

conservatism fueled the counterrevolutionary aspect of his own thought. The American exemption from premodern history and the implications for government and economics further deepened his analysis. Chambers concluded that America, capitalist from its founding, represented the "breathless acceleration" contained in the free market system.[53] The absence of an aristocratic class with its wealth and title bound in the nation's soil and history meant that the energy of the market had never met solid opposition, at least until the Progressive era. Even the government itself was not immune, according to Chambers; its capture by the forces of industry had produced the War Between the States and the consequent subjugation of the seceding Southern states.[54] The heritage of America was that of flux and constant development. Thus, appeals to conservatism were inherently problematic within the American tradition.

The Cartesian quality of reasoning performed almost unconsciously by the individual American fortified Chambers's analysis of America's practice of experimentation and invention.[55] Resembling the attempts by French philosopher René Descartes to erect human thinking on the plane of geometric certainty, the American had taken this philosophical thought in the manner befitting his own habit of being. While other Western nations both benefited and were hindered by centuries of experiences across wide ranges of thought, politics, and religion, the United States had no past to overcome or to reject—and no sure future to embrace. The American's future was dynamic. It was a dynamism to which the American looked, and in which he believed with unyielding certainty. Prudence and caution before moments and opportunities of great change were foreign to the American, convinced as he was of the rightness of his own mind and its preconceived conclusions.

If America's essence was that of "creative destruction" Chambers's conclusion for American conservatism was straightforward in its logic: a conservatism that sought to apply the brakes on the fearful changes of capitalism was at odds with the essence of the American polity. Chambers's response was to "retard for an instant . . . hold back lest the rush of development (in a multitude of frightful forms) carry us to catastrophe."[56] The sober recognition in this statement paid justice to the realities of modernity, seeking to provide mercy where possible, while eschewing any fantastic belief in impossible alternatives.

Conservatism's larger task, Chambers contended, was to understand the razor-wire act thrust upon it at that specific moment in history. In particular, Chambers writes:

> Those who remain in the world, if they will not surrender on its terms, must maneuver within its terms. That is what conservatives must decide: how much to give in order to survive at all; how much to give in order not to give up the basic principles. And, of course, that results in a dance along a precipice.[57]

Chambers commented favorably on Ohio Senator Robert Taft and his prudential abilities at holding back "the rush of development" at opportune times. Curiously, while Taft was seen as an old-line conservative supporting the gospel of small government, non-interventionism, and free markets amidst the surge of the encompassing federal state, Chambers described him as a man operating within a complex of swift evolution and spiraling force.[58] Taft could not help but be a classical liberal moving, as he did, in the most modern of nations within the most modern of centuries. In such circumstances, conservatism as a principle was almost non-existent. This was no idiosyncratic judgment, Chambers noted, for Taft himself understood the constraints of his moment and merely diverted the elevator from reaching the highest floor.

The measure of success was to create new opportunities for transformation within society by principles no longer seen as self-evidently true or worthy of popular acceptance. Here, Taft and his signature piece of legislation, the Taft-Hartley Act of 1947, provided an appealing example of "the cliff dancers" who "dance along a precipice" and attempt to breathe liberty into yet another realm of personal freedom that was endangered by state action. The Taft-Hartley Act, of course, restricted more coercive tools of labor unions and permitted the possibility of states passing right-to-work laws. Taft-Hartley helped preclude a more vigorous union-ism establishing itself in American industry. The effectual truth in Chambers's mind was the space preserved by the legislation for liberty to re-emerge in this sphere. If individuals in modern democracies largely accepted the Marxist understanding that viewed the relationship between worker and owner as antagonistic, and a sure deprivation of material prosperity absent state regulation, then an appropriate conservative response was to re-present the goods that flowed from the freedom of contract and the mobility of labor and capital. In time, through the space made possible by Taft and other conservative leaders, other favorable realities might intrude, producing a much needed correction to statist overreach. In his acts of responsible political force, in particular, the Taft-Hartley Act, Taft was one of "the cliff dancers" who created room within which freedom could still breathe. For Chambers, Taft was a model of responsible statesmanship, securing favorable outcomes in otherwise distressing political situations.

Defining Principles

Looking to respond decisively to author-philosopher Ayn Rand, William F. Buckley Jr. printed Chambers's review of Rand's novel *Atlas Shrugged* in *National Review.* Entitled "Big Sister is Watching You," Chambers's review turned his philosophical framework previously employed against Communism on Ayn Rand's "Objectivism." One sees again how Chambers's concerns with the modern era shaped his response not simply to Communism but to other political issues as well.

Several commentators have noted that Chambers's review effectively stopped Rand from having any significant impact on the growing conservative movement, and that the review ensured Rand's Objectivism was relegated to the periphery of the Right in America, with her agenda never receiving the critical support she desired. This view may not be accurate for a number of reasons. First of all, Rand probably never wanted to be a part of the type of conservatism advanced by *National Review* or the broader movement it was attempting to spearhead. Further, it is doubtful that the period's nascent conservatism would ever have accepted Randian Objectivism. In addition to finding liberation from collectivist economics, Rand, who found her ideal in Aristotelian ethics, but frequently sounded like a rock-ribbed Nietzschean, looked for man to break from certain classical and theological virtues that many conservatives were pointing towards as essential components of a free society.

The devastating strike that Chambers made, however, by linking Rand's thought to a materialist philosophy was his diagnosis of the manner she affected throughout *Atlas Shrugged*. Success, happiness, and achievement by the novel's heroes all consist in material production, technological accomplishment, and monetary profits, not to mention their sexual gymnastics, all occurring in the noticeable absence of children. Chambers analyzed the novel in the following terms:

> *Atlas Shrugged* can be called a novel only by devaluing the term. . . . Its story merely serves Miss Rand to get the customers inside the tent, and as a soapbox to deliver her Message. The Message is the thing. It is, in sum, a forthright philosophic materialism. Upperclassmen might incline to sniff and say that the author has, with vast effort, contrived a simple materialist system, one, intellectually, at about the stage of the oxcart, though without mastering the principle of the wheel. Like any consistent materialism, this one begins by rejecting God, religion, original sin, etc. Thus, Randian Man, like Marxist Man, is made the center of a godless world.[59]

The principle mischief in the book for Chambers was its proclamation of salvation through capitalism, a salvation that Rand proclaimed with ideological certainty.[60]

Chambers understood capitalism and individual liberty as necessary aspects of the limited, finite human person, permitting his mistakes, follies, and successes to find balance and concord amid the wide-ranging choices of persons. But Rand inverted this order, so he believed. Liberty and capitalism in Rand's fiction are absolute forces promising solutions to existential dilemmas. The understanding of the human person in the classical philosophical-theological consensus was nullified. In capitalism, here conceived as a vast, impersonal force and order, a system without sacrificial love or mercy, the person realized in a state of masterful sovereignty over self and others not similarly clever or acquisitive.

The detriment such an order posed to the human spirit was easy to discern, according to Chambers. His analysis concluded that Rand merely offered another godless materialism. Chambers observed in his review, "For the world, as seen in a materialist view from the Right, scarcely differs from the same world seen in materialist view from the Left. The question becomes chiefly: who is to run that world in whose interests, or perhaps, at best, who can run it more efficiently?"[61] Self-interest becomes despotic when it is no longer governed by the higher and nobler obligations of love, sacrifice, and the numerous loyalties that exist in a humane society. Chambers believed that absent conviction about the required goods for a noble life freedom becomes subdued by the compulsion of stronger interests. Unable to define the content of human freedom apart from a narrow conception of self-interest, the amputation of the person was inevitable given the pride, selfishness, and vanity of the human will.

Chambers's legendary blow against Rand came from his insistence that not only was she peddling a suffocating materialism but she shouted it in a tone that brooked no dissent. That is, the peculiar prisons of ideological thought were again in the offering. This time, they lurked in the pen of a Russian émigré. Terms of engagement were being put forward that defined a new man while ridiculing those few circumspect persons who would not be so defined. On the novel's imagination Chambers expounded:

> It consistently mistakes raw force for strength, and the rawer the force, the more reverent the posture of the mind before it. It supposes itself to be the bringer of a final revelation. Therefore, resistance to the message cannot be tolerated because disagreement can never be merely honest, prudent or just humanly fallible (dissent from revelation so final can only be willfully wicked). There are ways of dealing with such wickedness, and, in fact, right reason itself enjoins them. From almost any page of *Atlas Shrugged,* a voice can be heard, from painful necessity, commanding: "To a gas chamber—go."[62]

Finally, Chambers instructed, one should not "place much confidence in the diagnosis of a doctor who supposed that the Hippocratic Oath was a kind of curse."[63] If Chambers's attempted construction of a counterrevolutionary program leaves an impression of undue pragmatism and flexibility, his review of Rand's *Atlas Shrugged* was a statement of conservative strictures that must be upheld. From the dissection of Rand one returns to Chambers's view that the knotted conundrums of thought in the modern world were the evidence of the distortions that arose from modernity's declamations of faith and reason. Healing these wounds was the main project of conservatism. However, the task of the statesman and the requirements of prudence still called for proper attention. This, too, Chambers attempted to provide.

This proclamation of conservative spirit and the goods that must be upheld in the contest with Communism found similar expression in Chambers's critique of the Austrian economist Ludwig von Mises's book *The Anti-Capitalist Mentality*.[64] Mises believed that the energy driving the loathing of capitalism was the intellectual class's envy of the power the system delivered to the businessmen, moneychangers, and tastes of the common man. Barred from having imperious cultural, social, and political power, the intellectuals constantly pressed for capitalism's replacement with various socialist alternatives, so that the purported expert, and no one else, can dictate the cultural, social, and political mores. Hence, jealousy of the classical-liberal order, with its de-emphasis of politics and ideology in favor of commercial exchange, drove the intellectuals' voracious appetites for socialist reform.

Chambers found Mises's attribution of anti-capitalism to the phenomenon of envy a vast oversimplification that failed to weigh the aspirations and longings of the person that reacted in baffling ways to a materialist culture and society.[65] Seeing everything in terms of envy was itself dehumanizing, as it reduced the person to a collection of willed desires separated from wisdom. Not disputing the fact of envy, flourishing as it did in an age "where the Cadillac dangles always just out of reach at the end of the stick," Chambers pointed to its more dismal source in an age of secularism and materialism with its attendant anomie and apathy. Envy, in Chambers's mind, was an inseparable aspect of human motivations and actions; however, its presence was not necessarily suffocating or all-encompassing. The Soviet Communist or Western intellectual may envy the success, power, and possessions of a corporate businessman and his capitalist democracy, but their critiques asserted rationales far beyond that of envy.

At stake for Chambers was the human spirit, which materialism and secularism, not capitalism, denied. The conscience, Chambers argued, was not so easily placated, and continued to seek the full measure of man's being. Thus, envy, when properly understood, pulsated within a society that ascribed perverted values to certain appetites and desires to the exclusion of permanent longings that demanded higher fulfillment.[66] Missed by Mises's critique was the fundamental leveling of the bourgeois-capitalist order, not by a rival system of economic control, but by the prophetic jeremiad of rationalism that asserted a new order of goods that allegedly spoke to the human person at the point where capitalism ended or was incapable of going with its own narrative.

The socialist intellectual pontificated a slip-shod historical understanding made worse by an errant view of the person, but the fine point of his analysis drew blood because it asserted positively a vision of the requirements necessary for human fulfillment. The Trotskyite, the Marxist, and the socialist were making claims to justice that were terminal, separating, as it did, the wheat from the chaff. Their opponents languished in facts, empirical evidence of falling prices for formerly scarce goods, ample supplies of commodities, and the intensifying array of advanced consumer goods, luxury items, and conveniences in the capitalist system. While these claims were hard to dismiss, and were in their own manner evidence of a superior catallaxy, the socialist intellectual merely doubled down on his theoretical weapons, hurling them at the peculiar listlessness of individuals living in the prosperous West.

This observation was a key tenet in Chambers's overall canon of Western declinism typified by its inability to assess and counter the threat of Communism. As such, Chambers critiqued Mises's reliance on envy as one that was not wrong conclusively but one that, by placing undue emphasis on social manifestations, failed to uncover fully the profoundly disconcerting aspects of the modern West.

One sees in these assessments of Mises and Rand the final signs of Chambers's conservatism and the enduring qualities that it must give voice to within the particular milieu it is placed. The basic lie of the ideological regime was not located, in the first instance, in a failure to produce wealth, but in its undermining of the human person's primary experiences with the good itself. In this vein, Chambers was part of a larger collection of twentieth century thinkers for whom misshaped material realities pointed towards larger deformations in the spirit of man. Thus, like the insights provided by Pope John Paul II of the gross distortions of the Communist imperium, Chambers wanted to reassert the ontological dignity of the human person through a conservative program that kept alive these ancient truths by restating them in a new era. Chambers, ultimately, would have no part of a conservative program that did not take its directions from *la fine pointe de l'âme* and find the terminus of man's actions in the providence of God and the chain of grace extended to man throughout the centuries.

CHAPTER FIVE

THE ASCENT FROM MODERNITY

For Chambers, the recovery of the West's primary truths needed to extend past the Continental Enlightenment's conceit that man constructs his own reality through an overarching reason.[1] The piercing counsel of *Witness* was that the West must reject Communism in the name of something other than modern liberalism and its foundation in the principles of Enlightenment rationalism. In certain sections of *Witness* Chambers proclaims that Communism is the effectual truth of philosophical modernity. The crucial element in a recovery from Communism would be the rearticulation of an understanding of the human person fulfilled by ordered goods that transcend the human will. The concept of a participation in a changeless reality that speaks to man in his innermost person, giving him an awareness of his nature and purpose through self-reflection, were essential to this articulation. Chambers's belief that man's nature required God for its resolution was refined by insights from the Protestant Reformation, Søren Kierkegaard, Karl Barth, and Reinhold Niebuhr, among others.

Chambers's writing reflected a profound admiration for the thickness of human liberty when tied to the moral contents of life. Man's liberty, however, is also one of self-reflection, born from the direct experience of liberty as the organizing principle of man's life, enabling him to live for goodness and truth. Caught between the desire to know the purpose of his limited existence and the craving to transcend all limitations, man acutely experiences the singularity of his being. Stemming from the nature of his soul, man's fundamental tensions erupt with frequency and ferocity.

The balm to this tempestuousness is the formal acknowledgment of the sheer contingency of one's being, the open recognition that man always stands in need of God if he is to know himself truly. Chambers held that the greatness of a civilization, a society, and a nation always began with the sincere attempt to answer the question of who is man and what must he exalt and worship. Chambers's counsel, as fresh as it was ancient, was man's need for divinity such that his thinking and striving knew their sure foundation, for without this foundation man's dignity fades from his recognition.

Chambers's struggle originated in his existential embrace of the tremendous intellectual and moral deceptions of totalitarian ideology. From the open civilizational "wound" of Nazi and Soviet crimes, and the intellectual refusal or inability of Western elites to condemn the Soviet horrors, Chambers looked to the forgotten possibility of redemptive suffering and its lessons. Confronting ideological nihilism with the hope of reclaiming partially obscured, yet necessary, goods required the imagination to contemplate the graced approach to truth and the will to reveal it. Chambers

rejected the dialectical materialist formulation of Marxist-Lenin-
ism, whereby affliction is an acceptable, even necessary step toward
human maturity consummated by the preeminent Communist
regime. Instead, Chambers saw suffering as an attempt to exist as
a moral and spiritual entity. To be among the cast of violent char-
acters and events rendered by Communist ideology, and yet affirm
life as a moral and spiritual complex, was the heroic course. Man
suffers, in Chambers's terms, because there is no other humane
path left to him in the twentieth century.[2]

Chambers affirmed that in brokenness man comes to find his
telos (final purpose). Understanding that happiness is not a suf-
ficient purpose of his existence, man recognizes that responsibility
for himself and those he loves is the real challenge. Chambers cast
his own complexity into the throes of his conscience, making
sense of his mysterious wanderings through a participation in an
order above his own will. Chambers viewed happiness, at least the
happiness of modern man's constant craving, as an illusory good,
because it had been severed from a life of courage and humility.

Chambers's evocation of the limited, conditioned nature
of human knowledge and action provided an outline of a sure
approach to the givens of the human person and how these should
inform political rule in the modern, liberal order. While the
application of this insight requires prudence and adjustment, the
standards Chambers enunciated with lyrical voice and complete
self-effacement hold true in every age. Chambers held that the
goods that drive and shape human action and civilization serve as
the touchstones of practical judgment and action in any age, and
exist above the human will.

Chambers insistently proclaimed that social, political, and economic problems, so acute in the late-modern era, are never the ultimate quandaries. Rather, they are the inevitable outcomes of the failure to accord man his full measure in the authentic tones of spiritual and philosophical realism. The severity of Chambers's guidance, as judged by the contemporary intellect, is a reflection of our misplaced being, emancipated from its natural requirements of ordered thought and ordered existence under God. Unwilling to perceive and reflect on the essence of the human person, the modern finds himself confused by someone who did precisely this and urged its conclusions upon his troubled scene.

Sense, Sensibility, and Liberal Anti-Communism

The disconsolation at Chambers's criticism of his political age and the image of man that informed it was evident in the contemporary responses offered by two different groups of intellectuals: the liberal anti-Communists and the anti-anti-Communists.[3] Many liberal anti-Communist thinkers made qualified evaluations of Chambers, but resisted the full-throated denouncements found in many newspapers and journals of the period. Most liberal anti-Communist writers regarded Chambers as truthful in the main, correct in his accusations that Alger Hiss had spied for the Soviet Union, that other federal officials had performed similar activities, and that important figures in the New Deal had acted in less than reputable manners by ignoring, not noticing, or even covering up such treason. The publication of *Witness,* however, complicated greatly their acceptance of his claims.

In *Witness* Chambers enlarged his claims considerably, so

much so that many liberal supporters saw him as the spearhead of the strike against the Progressive New Deal. Instead of posing a serious challenge to the power and nature of Soviet Communism, Chambers became the intellectual workhorse in a wave of revanchist right-wing politics. Under this formulation, liberal acceptance of Chambers became the acceptance of Richard Nixon, the House Committee on Un-American Activities, the rising conservative movement, and Senator Joseph McCarthy. This was a political reality far too difficult to digest for even those sympathetic towards Chambers. While notable in this respect, the tepid acceptance by many liberal anti-Communists of Chambers's accusations portended their ultimate judgment of the essence of his position and its fullest implications for the political thought of the modern Left.

The dialogue that ensued between Chambers and this group of writers and thinkers performed the estimable function of revealing the fundamental controversies at stake in postwar American intellectual and political life. The trenchancy of Chambers's analysis of modern ideology was inescapably clear. Of course, the reach of his criticism was the crux of the engagement, accusing not just Communist ideology but liberalism and socialism as its anterior dialectical partners. Chambers, however, did not stay in the domain of theory exclusively, but connected misdeeds and political tactics with Leftist theory itself.[4] A man who had, in 1939, given evidence to Adolf Berle, the Assistant Secretary of State of the State Department, regarding Communist activities by federal employees in government departments and agencies throughout the New Deal, Chambers was not reticent in proclaiming how these treasonous acts were so widespread and so glaringly ignored.

For Chambers, the New Deal was a revolutionary political movement relative to the principles and history of American constitutional governance. The ideals of the New Deal did not issue from the American experience proper, but were an attempt to actualize collectivist principles, owing to new theories of economics, constitutions, law, and the evolving notion of the person that these were built to explain and master.[5] Recalling his own experiences in the Soviet Underground, Chambers noted, "It is surprising how little I knew about the New Deal, although it had been all around me during my years in Washington. But all the New Dealers I had known were Communists or near-Communists. None of them took the New Deal seriously as an end in itself. They regarded it as an instrument for gaining their own revolutionary ends."[6] Compounded by several events Chambers encountered as informant, the force of this observation rose above the merely time-bound observation of idealistic Communists working in the New Deal to include the theoretical trajectory of the modern liberal project.

In the case of treasonous New Dealers, their ease in working in government service with loyal federal officials indicated to Chambers the transformative stature of Roosevelt's domestic policies. That both groups saw themselves working in the same general political direction was no mere coincidence. Chambers held that this latter point was brought into greater relief by the abject refusal of many New Deal officials to comprehend and admit the guilt of Hiss and other New Deal servants. After all, the accusations of treason had been conveyed to Adolf Berle, and they had gone unheeded.[7] Another point that impressed itself on Chambers was the sheer number of federal employees willing to inform on their government to him, as well as other underground agents serving in Washington, DC.

Chambers offered this assessment on the inability of key New Dealers to account for the presence of Communists within federal operations:

> The New Deal was a genuine revolution, whose deepest purpose was not simply reform within existing traditions, but a basic change in the social, and, above all, the power relationships within the nation.. . . . It was a revolution by bookkeeping and lawmaking. In so far as it was successful, the power of politics had replaced the power of business. . . . It was only of incidental interest that the revolution was not complete, that it was made not by tanks and machine guns, but by acts of Congress and decisions of the Supreme Court.[8]

New Deal liberals, possessed with humanitarian motives and aims of general social uplift, were unable to register the Communists within their midst because of a partially shared ideology. The possibilities of reaching new heights of social evolution through centralized planning, nationalized regulatory policies, diminishment of property rights, and expansive views of federal power over commerce, were held by both groups. Thus, the failure to recognize Communist maneuvering in and around the departments and agencies administering the New Deal was nearly inevitable given the thrust of the age's political idealism. Pursuing his analysis further, Chambers noted:

For as between revolutionists who only half know what they are doing and revolutionists who know exactly what they are doing the latter are in a superb maneuvering position. At the basic point of the revolution—the shift of power from business to government—the two kinds of revolutionists were at one; and they shared many other views and hopes. Thus men who sincerely abhorred the word Communism, in the pursuit of common ends found that they were unable to distinguish Communists from themselves, except that it was just the Communists who were likely to be most forthright and most dedicated in the common cause. . . . For men who could not see that what they firmly believed was liberalism added up to socialism could scarcely be expected to see what added up to Communism. Any charge of Communism enraged them precisely because they could not grasp the differences between themselves and those against whom it was made.[9]

The curious turn Chambers described was not that New Deal liberals thought they were explicitly being named by him as Communists, but that the Communists he did name possessed political aims largely inseparable from their own. They concluded, therefore, that Chambers must be lying. His charges were dismissed by those who had too much to lose politically from the exposure of their own gross naïveté, or, as some believed, of their complicity in treason and betrayal of their country.

This immediate, intense reaction against Chambers was motivated by the need to preserve the integrity and purity of American liberalism and its chief product, the New Deal. No one better exemplified the animating ideals of this progressive turn in American politics than Alger Hiss. Perfect in academic pedigree, Hiss's record of high-level career service and dedication personified the enlightened civil servant ethos of Progressive-era politics. Hiss held firmly to Progressivism's expansionist vision of federal government power and its internationalist humanitarianism. Therefore, if Hiss could fall victim to Chambers, then much else was also at stake.

Diana Trilling's essay entitled "A Memorandum on the Hiss Case" provided one of the firmest rejoinders to Chambers's schematic of theoretical liberalism. In the essay, Trilling advanced the common sense proposition that liberalism itself would not, ultimately, stand or fall with the fortunes of Alger Hiss.[10] Moreover, Trilling reiterated that American liberalism, a response to the fundamental challenges of governance in the twentieth century, provided no inherent halfway house on the road to political radicalism. She was, however, quite sensitive to liberalism's susceptibility to an idealism that left it unable to morally comprehend the *pathos* of Communism. Trilling's essay, which intended to rehabilitate American liberalism against the charges of Chambers and other conservative anti-Communists, danced around many of Chambers's finer points, even submitting to certain indictments.[11]

Trilling stated that American liberalism during the Popular Front era had looked largely with affection to the Soviet Union for the resistance it could offer against Nazism. The antifascist front, directed in crucial ways by Moscow, was seen by Western liberals through their own prism of purified intentions. Aiming to combat the vicious hatred of Nazi power, idealistic liberals accorded a certain angelic status to radical Leftists throughout the decade, regarding their own democratic governments as weak and confused in responding to fascism.[12] Thus, Trilling argued, it came to pass that liberals found their own idealism in the socialism of the Popular Front, whose members in many nations were led by the Soviet Union.[13] Trilling remarked:

> I think we can also say that in our own century the source of all political idealism has been socialism, and, since the Russian Revolution, specifically the socialism of the Soviet Union. I do not mean that whoever has worked for political progress has necessarily been a socialist. I mean only that it has been from socialist theory that political progress has chiefly taken its inspiration, and from the socialist example its practice.[14]

The goals of political action across many democracies in the 1930s, including America, were substantive equality, extensive commercial regulation and taxation, and vast social service provisioning—with all of this, ultimately, guided by an idealism anchored in socialist thought.

Under this line of reasoning the treasonous nature of Hiss's acts were expurgated. Instead, they were viewed as a species of loyalty to the higher laws of history and ideology that attempted to serve conscience, but, ultimately, undid or subverted it.[15] According to many Western liberals, in serving the Soviet Union and Communism Hiss had fulfilled his true end, the end of universalized man. Therefore, betrayal of something as concrete and particular as one's country was not a worthy objection. Hiss's innocence was never a simple matter of facts and evidence; constitutional oaths, trusts and responsibilities had been transcended by higher planes of ideological faith. This creed, Hiss's supporters sensed, was the real issue being contested by the Hiss case and the ensuing war of opinion. As Leslie Fiedler commented on the Hiss liberals, "Maybe at the bottom of their hearts, they did not finally want him to admit anything, but preferred the chance he gave them to say: he is, we are, innocent."[16] The "liberalism of responsibility" that Chambers's accusations ushered in was not an easily forgiving reality regarding the past acts of Leftist ideologues.

By her own parsing of the assumptions made by the contemporary Left, Trilling offered further commentary that was unintentionally supportive of Chambers's wide philosophical cuts against liberalism. Trilling taught that within liberalism there ranged two camps, seemingly inseparable, but divided on the most crucial issue of the day. The liberal anti-Communists set their faces directly against the Soviet Union and its malicious ideology, while liberals proper judged themselves by their willingness to tolerate certain features of Communism.[17] Trilling contended that the foolishness of the latter liberal doctrine was a sentimental ignorance, comfortably resting in idealism's lily-feathered nest. Immune to the time-honored lessons of power, whose importance was amplified in the political contests of the twentieth century, the liberal was disconnected from the consequences of his own assumptions about politics and power.

Chambers was prescient concerning the writhing anger liberals directed against him, saying, "Every move against the Communists was felt by the liberals as a move against themselves. If only for the sake of their public health record, the liberals, to protect their power, must seek as long as possible to conceal from themselves and everybody else the fact that the government had been Communist-penetrated."[18] But the thought necessarily intrudes that Chambers's analytical collapse of New Deal liberalism into the orbit of Leftist radicalism was an overreach. Chambers writes, "when I aimed at Communism, I also hit something else. What I hit was the forces of that great socialist revolution, which, in the name of liberalism, spasmodically, incompletely, somewhat formlessly, but always in the same direction, has been inching its ice cap over the nation for two decades."[19]

Certainly the results of the New Deal were less significant in their social-democratic achievements when compared to those of other Western democracies. Much of the early and most statist legislation of the period was turned back by the Supreme Court. Even the famous "switch in time that saved nine," which marked the end of the ascent of Roosevelt's domestic political agenda, resulted mostly in a more expansive view of the Constitution's commerce clause. This enlargement of the commerce clause's reach, the further instantiation of the administrative state, and the social insurance provisioning in Social Security remain the enduring legacies of the New Deal. This political vision is obviously not the Founders' Constitution, and these developments placed important milestones toward an expansive federal government, eliminating the inlaid, constitutional limits to its power. Nevertheless, a revolution did not occur.

Chambers's analysis of the New Deal and the dubiety of many of its central political and administrative leaders towards

Communist infiltration is not easily refuted by the mere recitation of the period's more moderate and enduring liberal reforms. To understand Chambers's charge one must view it in the full light of his intimate and sustained political commitments and the manner in which he communicated them. In both his service of the Communist Party in the Soviet Underground and in his later testimony against past Communist espionage, Chambers revealed his abiding, almost universalist desire to use political action to fire the temporal order with justice. The truth of this observation is deepened by a glimpse into Chambers's writings. In these works, Chambers uses a robust theological, literary, and philosophical lens to interpret for his age both Communism and the lighter shades of Leftist ideology less explicitly identified with it.

Chambers attempted to connect his age to its disregarded truths through theology, philosophy, and literature, obscured as they were by the ideological *putsch* (revolt) of modernist ideology. In *Witness* Chambers communicated the depth of his own fall into Communism and his redemptive rise from it through parallels with, and references to, classical and modern literature, Old and New Testament figures, the voices of Protestant theology, and existentialist philosophy. A list of these figures and works includes the following: Jonah, the raising of Lazarus, *The Divine Comedy, Macbeth,* John Milton's *Samson Agonistes,* Ludwig van Beethoven's *Ninth Symphony, Les Misérables,* George Fox's spiritual writings, Fyodor Dostoyevsky's *The Possessed,* and selected poems of the German poet, Rainer Maria Rilke. In correspondence with both Buckley and Toledano Chambers interpreted the conflict with Hiss and Communism as a personal and universal exemplification of the Greek tragedian view of the human condition as one of unavoidable strife and death.

Seen by many American writers as a Dostoyevskian figure, "un-American . . . or at least un-Anglo-Saxon" in his prosaic and literal intensity, Chambers worked out his diagnosis of late modernity in the language of writer and poet.[20] Devoted to the image of God in man that had been defaced by him and others under the spellbinding claims of ideology, the theological and moral vision of great literature became the form of his own treatment of the modern mind. While not denying the penetrating, if not convincing, prescriptions Chambers gave regarding the development of political conservatism in America and Soviet statecraft, his soulful grappling with political ideology contains the clearest and most enduring elements of his writing.

The structure of *Witness* itself stands as a modern parallel to Dante's monumental *Divine Comedy*. Chambers does not journey through a literal Hell and Purgatory on his way to Paradise, but he does walk through their modern equivalents of broken and dislocated families, proletarian-ized citizens from the streets of Baltimore and New Orleans, the utterly forsaken dignity of post World War I Germans, and that most modern of hells, ideological Communism and its redemptive promises. This personal excursion into hell exacted its own terrible price, but like Dante, Chambers returned from the innermost terrace of the Inferno. As the French writer and statesman André Malraux told Chambers, "You are one of those who did not return from Hell with empty hands." Indeed, Chambers used the imagery and allusions of rebirth and redemption as rungs of his existential ladder to inform the reader of his ascent from Communism's *gnostic* hell. Similar to Dante, who upon emerging from Hell and Purgatory reports that he sees the stars, Chambers, after detailing the full contents of his life to the Federal Bureau of Investigation, wrote, *"E quindi uscimmo a riveder le stelle"* (And so we emerged again to see the stars).[21] Having spent much of his life inside modernity's effectual truth—Communism—Chambers returned to the living with even stranger truths to communicate.

At the beginning of *Witness* Chambers recalled his rebirth: "When we dead awaken. . . ."[22] His rising was like Lazarus's own regeneration. Chambers had been raised by the spirit, apart from his own will or desires consumed, as they were, in suffocating errors. The new life given his dry bones, Chambers held, was not his own—a fact he knew all too well when he began his flight from the Soviet Underground.[23]

Broadening Chambers's experience was his own commitment to the Swiss Reformed theologian Karl Barth and his central observation that "[m]an cannot define God by talking about man, in however loud a voice. God is *ganz anders*—wholly different." Joining Barth's idea with Kierkegaard's insight that man's limited, finite purposes are infinitely separated from the ways of God, Chambers communicated his radical debt to providential grace that had chosen him for its own purposes. Chambers believed that a total response was called for, not because of its rationality or intelligibility, but owing to man's overwhelming need for God, a need that became intensely personal. Chambers connected man's need for God to the story of Solon's weeping for his dead son—the only possible response Solon relates to inexplicable tragedy.[24] Solon, the Athenian democratic legislator and poet, was asked by a friend, "Why do you weep since it cannot help?" Solon replied: "That is why I weep—because it cannot help."[25] Solon had to suffer and mourn in response to his son's death. The paradoxical nature of man's being demanded suffering in response to the loss of the good. If joy and love marked its presence, the absence of the possibility of suffering meant the loss of meaning. Man's limited and finite being could no longer hope for anything beyond its conditioned experience. Comparatively, Chambers reasoned, man also had to find God as the necessary foundation of his being. There simply was no other way to an authentic existence. To contemplate this truth was to begin to experience love.

Witness also stands as an American instance of Fyodor Dostoevsky's *The Possessed*, the Russian novelist's attempt to take his own stand against revolutionary ideology in nineteenth century Russia.[26] Understanding the conflict as one that would impose final terms between Communism and freedom Chambers argued that Communism was the enemy of the image of God in man. The resolute Christian writer had drawn his bead on the enemy relying on an appeal to the imagination of Christian Humanism as his chief offensive weapon.

The Strange Endurance of Communism

At the age of thirty-one Chambers quit a promising career as an author, poet, and translator for a position in the Soviet Underground. The actual clandestine duties he performed only added to the strength of his commitments.[27] A man who many believed could have entered the highest echelon of American prose writers substantially reduced his literary career for the role of courier and contact, shuttling often inconsequential documents to faceless, nameless agents. Chambers the spy offered up his talents for the purpose of serving the revolution he loved, even if it meant the performance of duties of a rather menial nature. In time, he came to lead a cell of important federal officials, but this specific role was not the motivating factor in Chambers's decision to become an underground agent. Chambers's Communist actions and his later decision to become an informant reflected his belief that action emerged from and was connected to the existential commitment the soul had made to truth.

In confronting Communism root and branch, Chambers produced the synopsis of the modern dialectic of political thought and its strange course towards the armed doctrines of totalitarianism. In seeing Communism as the chief output of a regime of thought stretching back to the Continental Enlightenment, if not to a Renaissance anthropology, Chambers exposed the theoretical errors of modernity. Chambers's writings presented modernity's more dismal aspects as the results of its series of separations, of religion from politics, truth from liberty, wisdom from reason, and power from opinion.

Modernity's enduring contribution has been to impose on man severe cognitive limitations to his ability to grasp truth or to understand the natural ground of his being. Man's scope of knowledge and action are reduced by the concomitant diminishment of philosophy from having any capacity to speak to the natural wonder of man. Further, in the modern estimation, man's religious sentiments become inherently private concerns. Religion tends toward irrelevance, unable to interpose serious contributions to the civil and social order. Consequently, the complex and mysterious nature of man is dismissed, for any purportedly scientific reason. Incapable of final dismissal, however, man's nature still seeks reflection in the social ordering of normative goods that emerge from man's participation in the eternal realm by thought and religious exercise.

No longer sure of man's communion with God, the exclusivity of worldly reality becomes unavoidable. Without the possibility of a mediative participation of the divine, man is left with the need to define away his limited existence in favor of ideological transcendence. Chambers recorded that it was precisely this dialectic between Communism and freedom in the American mind that was at stake in the Hiss case: "At heart, the Great Case was this critical conflict of faiths . . . two irreconcilable faiths of our time—Communism and Freedom—came to grips in the persons of two conscious and resolute men."[28] One might observe that Hiss, as well as Chambers, believed himself an apostle of freedom, advancing man's freedom through the logic of Communism. That is, in its grasp was the true Enlightenment overcoming the falsities of the bourgeois freedoms of capitalism, democracy, virtue, and religion.

Moving further into the errors of modern thought Chambers acutely described the new role of worldly transformation that Marx assigned to philosophy.[29] The life of wonder, the desire to know the whole precisely because man's soul desires such pursuits, becomes non-sensible, a delusion from the central object of making the final man. Knowledge becomes power because knowledge is unable to possess the moral contents of life or to provide man with sure intellectual prerequisites to order his life as a rational being.

This statement of Marxist faith is completely reasonable in reference to the separations of modernity and the harsh barriers to authentic knowledge that it constructs. If man's purposes are thoroughly immanent, then it stands that reason must be employed in the unlocking of man's potentialities for temporal greatness. As Chambers indicated, "It is the vision of man's mind displacing God as the creative intelligence of the world. It is the vision of man's liberated mind, by the sole force of its rational intelligence, redirecting man's destiny and reorganizing man's life and the world."[30] Man must define what it means to be man and to define who, among the full range of persons, meets these criteria. Alongside this task is the organization of the world against those refusing the imposed ideological vision. Through the process of this ideological mechanism man sanctifies the temporal by the force of his own will.

Those rejecting the redirection of "man's destiny" were to become subject to the most uncompromising of judgments and fates. They were handed death and imprisonment by new gods— totalitarian regimes—who claimed to understand the intricate movements of history and the precise import these events had for the future. To resist the metaphysical regime on whose behalf history was now laboring amounted to a refusal to join the new community of man. One thereby became less than human, choosing against the new criterion of human excellence. In displacing God, and the classical and biblical sources of the Western intellectual tradition, the ideologue stood bare, possessed only of himself, and composed the god-like pronouncements that demanded, in time, nothing less than revolution, mass murder, and total war.

These are the movements of an age under the firm, unyielding claims of self-sovereignty and its related denouncements of the tragic notion that the human person carries inherent perversities of pride, arrogance, cruelty, and inordinate desires. Chambers saw that at the heart of the denial of God and of man's capacity for evil was a fatal declamation against liberty. Communists not only stood *for* something; they also stood *against* man's ability to reason, choose, and act under the guidance of his conscience. Without the possibility of choosing excellence man becomes equally unable to choose evil. Liberty is no longer a reality. Marx's impact is unavoidable on this score, contending as he did that man is a historically constructed being, substantively actualized by materialist forces outside of his control.

Self-sovereignty's desecration of the ground of the liberal regime is further revealed in its express disavowal of classical philosophical thought and orthodox religion. The possibility of man instantiating in tradition the insights, purposes, and wonderment such disciplines might cultivate is lost to the age of ideology. Freedom, Chambers argued, is the need of the human soul, as such; it is the singular aspect of man's glory, the imaging of God in man.[31] The operations of the soul are evidence of its ontological freedom. The anxious striving of the human person throughout history towards the good, the true, and the beautiful are the confirmable pieces of evidence that man's chief glory would not be found in the return to the Marxist state of nature of full employment, egalitarian social conditions, and consumerist fulfillment.

Modern ideology theoretically denies man's innate liberty and his participation in the higher law. Chambers stated, "Political freedom, as the Western world has known it, is only a political reading of the Bible. Religion and freedom are indivisible. Without freedom the soul dies. Without the soul there is no justification for freedom."[32] Man is a unique being worthy of respect and love, because, in his freedom, he is able to choose God through faith, thus overcoming his deep-seated atavism and alienation, in which he finds himself. The soul becomes the primary feature of his existence, informing him of a deeper logic in his own being and the reality he inhabits.

Chambers's expression of the necessary and deeply complementary relationship of "religion and freedom" also encompasses more than biblical morality. "Religion" in this sense can incorporate the debts man senses, almost preternaturally, that he owes God, his creator and sustainer. For man, the being of imagination, reason, and wonder, senses that these capacities are gifts to him; hence, they serve a reality above his will. Religion is the possibility for human excellence, prominently displayed in man freely reverencing his author through these gifts.

In the contest for liberty Chambers emphasized the necessity of the spiritual aspect of man's being and its near-universal place in history.[33] The interior quality of man's existence seeks outer expression in the habits of sociality and action where man proclaims his allegiances:

> Communism is what happens when, in the name of Mind, men free themselves from God. But its view of God, its knowledge of God, its experience of God, is what alone gives character to a society or a nation, and meaning to its

destiny. Its culture, the voice of this character, is merely
that view, knowledge, experience, of God, fixed by its most
intense spirits in terms intelligible to the mass of men.
There has never been a society or a nation without God.
But history is cluttered with the wreckage of nations that
became indifferent to God, and died.[34]

While one can point to a train of civilizations that thrived apart
from a Christian understanding of God Chambers's statement is
broader, resting on the view that civilizations are led by and endure
because of the transcendent. The accumulated historical process
within a civilization of symbols, rites, and ceremonial displays is
the means whereby its citizens indicate to themselves the truth of
their individual and social existence. Communism's fatal logic is
seen in its attempt to bury this process of man.

The import of Chambers's remarks serves as a springboard for
reflection on the antitheist humanism and materialism that have
dominated the last three centuries of Western philosophy. Born out
of profound concern for the acting subject, modern thought has
insisted at every dialectical step upon the primacy of the individual.
Such thought was heroic in its initial strivings against an order that,
at crucial points, lacked the courage and imagination to understand
its own failures with regard to individual liberty, conflating the
order of authoritarian power with high virtue. However, on the path
to a noble freedom the emancipations of Enlightenment thought
somehow refused to cease. Rather, these accelerated outward and
upward, removing man from the heritage and legacies of Western
history. The moral reserves of mercy and sacrifice in premodern

thought were seemingly impossible in the newer mode of expression and self-understanding, and, as such, they were excluded by a modernity conscious of its own methodological atheism.

This broad shift in understanding informed the individual at the most fundamental level of his existence. The resistance of man's elevated sensibilities and religious longings, however, was sensed by Chambers and other anti-Communist thinkers. The death-dealing process that carried away the past habits, institutions, and cultural practices that had embodied and mediated transcendent longings did not rule unchecked. Man remained *homo orans* (the being who prays), and the sweep of modern philosophy and political thought was virtually powerless to explain the intractability of this feature of man.

Chambers's sensitivity to the impending cultural decline of a Western humanism cut off from the goods of classical thought and Christian theology emerged even more clearly after his death. The *stasis* of many liberal, Western democracies in the 1970s bore an uncomfortable connection to the problems in liberal thought as explored by Chambers. The loss of self-confidence Chambers identified in the West stemmed, he believed, from a thin conception of human freedom in secular democracy, one that was simultaneously disconnected from the transcendent objects of existence and coupled with an over-reliance on science and technology as the chief vehicles of existential understanding.

Of course, a crisis in confidence was perhaps more tolerable in a West that had endured world wars, depressions, and steep privations of basic goods. However, the irruption in America, Britain, and other Western states of a paralysis of confidence in the 1960s and

1970s was more troubling. Racked by mindless violence, strikes, rampant inflation, economic torpidity, and the rapid unfolding of sexual liberation, liberal democracy seemed to display, in acute form, the crisis of a material progress that had been severed from faith and freedom. Thus, the spirit of Chambers's brooding over the fate of the West retained relevance.

Chambers's grave admonitions that a victorious West may bear the imprint of its foe in a deeply philosophical and spiritual manner such that its image would be transformed into a materialist, atheist civilization haunted the West. The questions raised by theology and the anthropological understanding it inevitably points towards, as Chambers explicated, seemed palpable in a West rejected this time by its articulate young citizens, racial minorities, and the libertine ethos pulsating through its societies.

The uncomfortable facts behind the unrest of this period were the vast increases in wealth, comfort, and opportunity that had proliferated in the postwar West. These increases gathered baby-boomer families into a thick and protective economic and social web. Furthermore, the gains in justice for women and minorities, while delayed, were almost immeasurable from any standpoint in modern history. The most prosperous, well-fed, well-educated generation in Western history emerged to attack the very institutions and bourgeois norms that had undergirded their own comfortable upbringings and relatively peaceful societies. Surely, the social upheaval of the comparatively rich proved that Chambers was correct: more than abundant bread had to be in the offering to make freedom possible in the modern era.

Curiously, the West endured through the last three decades,

bolstered at key moments by a Polish pope, an American president, and a British prime minister, all of whom vigorously contested regnant liberal orthodoxies in their spheres of influence.[35] The continuance of the free West, as led by the United States, indicates that Chambers overlooked the West's deposits of moral reserves he felt it had rejected. Significant numbers of citizens in liberal democracies retained the capacity for thoughtful reflection and choice that continued to serve the ends of a humane civilization. While many leaders of the West refrained from serious consideration of the roots of their own civilization and what this history implied for governance, specific persons and groups within nations held the line at crucial points, listening to a former wisdom that still touched them.[36]

The last great victory of the twentieth century, the defeat of the Soviet Union and consequent liberation of millions, did not, as foretold in Chambers's writings, lead to something approaching a limitless peace and untrammeled prosperity. As argued in the first chapter, the victory produced no seismic shift in the West's self-understanding. An important but brief score of points was accorded to market economics and theoreticians of civil society and the principle of subsidiarity, but socialism, in crucial respects, has endured to present day.

Chambers's forbidding counsel against the philosophical foundations of Communism and the extensions of its assumptions about man, society, commerce, and government retains incredible power. Chambers saw the contest between Communism and Freedom as one between competing faiths: God or Man. This point of view struck writers of his period as Manichean and reductionist, yet the maintenance of this secular disdain towards writers of the spirit like Chambers becomes increasingly difficult to uphold in the face of challenges now issuing to humane civilization. Foremost in this regard was Chambers's connection of liberty to truth exhibited by man's participation in the order above his will.

A discrepancy emerges in Chambers's understanding given his reliance on a pure existentialist leap into faith and truth through an act of the will. Evidenced in parts of *Witness* where he recalls the dramatic pouring of his spirit towards God and away from Communism, Chambers's biography and thought do recall a certain identity with existentialism. The view expressed is that man might be unable to ever really understand his own turn from evil or nihilism. Man must rest content with himself and the utter inexplicability of his experiences. However, meaning and purpose, implicating reason and a certain comprehensibility of reality, loom throughout Chambers's conversion passages.

Chambers grasped that between premodern reason and modernist existentialism is the irresolvable tension, at a certain level, of being itself. Man may never fully understand all that he is, but this need not cover his choices with an unthinking voluntarism. Perhaps best expressed in Chambers's dual love for God and the image of God in man is a freedom joined to the human spirit given to it by God.

The listless freedom of the contemporary Westerner wanes before the rapid onset of new dissolutions. One piece of discomfiting evidence is the vanishing of the nuclear family and the nonexistence of a replacement birth rate in any Western nation, save for the United States. While strangely all sense the gravely destructive capabilities inherent in the regime of biotechnological medicine and therapy, there is the present inability to confront it with a thorough repudiation of its anti-human tendencies and purposes. The more beneficent promises of biotechnology, almost salvific in their proclamations, seem to exclude serious moral thought on the prospect that generations unborn may have their own liberty and self-understanding forever altered by the despotic power over human nature given by these new technologies. The Promethean impulse, latent in the modern project, as Chambers recognized, becomes explicit in the possibilities of limitless life exculpated from pain, suffering, and death. This diagnosis is troubling enough, apart from the culture of death and the cornerstone of right it has assumed in daily life, categorically removing entire persons from the protections of the law.

In the face of these developments, the dizzying intensity of Chambers's prescriptions remain. Chambers recognized that teaching moments for the West were increasingly rare and that, even when they occurred, intellectual stupor was often so deeply imbedded in men's minds that the insights of the moment were missed. Against the spirit of the mindless emancipations of man from God, of man from the community of men, and of man from the nature of his own person, is the mediation to man of the necessary goods of the human spirit.

Chambers saw Christ's climb up Golgotha as the clearest embodiment of wisdom; in this image, Chambers uncovers for the modern observer love and its call to man—that he leave behind the self to receive that which is above his own will. To redeem is then to offer witness. The man of sound mind who joins thought to sacrifice, unafraid to hang on his cross, is the man who advances a palpable hope that can again connect with the wonder of men. Chambers's writing remains because man needs truth along with beauty, to know that both are a part of his being. This is the gift Chambers left, and we, as always, are in need of it.

Notes

Chapter 1: The Project of a Counterrevolutionary

1. Alexander Pushkin, *The Bronze Horseman and Other Poems*, trans. D. M. Thomas (New York: Penguin Classics, 1983).

2. *Alger Hiss, Whittaker Chambers, and the Schism in the American Soul*, ed., Patrick A. Swan (Wilmington, DE: ISI Books, 2003). This edition compiles the best observations and writings from over four decades on the political and cultural meanings of the Hiss case. In addition the following works were published during the completion of this book that explore the differing and enduring contributions to American political life made by the Hiss case: Michael Kimmage's *The Conservative Turn: Lionel Trilling, Whittaker Chambers, and the Lessons of Anti-Communism* (Cambridge, MA: Harvard University Press, 2009) and Susan Jacoby's *Alger Hiss and the Battle for History* (New Haven, CT: Yale University Press, 2009). My assessment of these two books, "American Politics in the Age of the Exception," was featured in *Society*, 46, no. 5 (2009). While addressing many facts of Soviet espionage in America, John Earl Haynes, Harver Klehr, and Alexander Vassiliev's *Spies: the Rise and Fall of the KGB in America* (New Haven, CT: Yale University Press, 2009) offers stunning new evidence in

the first chapter on Hiss's guilt. The voluminous documentation by the authors in the form of Soviet intelligence cables and memos demonstrates that Alger Hiss was an active Soviet source inside the State Department until he left in 1946. Some of these documents also evince Soviet dismay at Hiss's and other federal government sources' compromised positions owing to Chambers's initial HUAC testimony in 1948.

3. Paul Kengor, *God and Ronald Reagan: A Spiritual Life* (New York: Harper Collins, 2004): 76–88. Ronald Reagan retained a sure confidence in Chambers's prescriptions from the moment he first read *Witness*. Reagan had entire passages of the autobiography suspended in his mind, often inserting them whole cloth into his speeches against Communism. While many elements informed Reagan's resolute anti-Communism, surely Chambers's narrative of conversion and identification of the anti–humanist essence of Communist ideology left its mark on Reagan's mind.

4. *The Solzhenitsyn Reader: New and Essential Writings* 1947–2005, ed., Edward E. Ericson, Jr. and Daniel J. Mahoney (Wilmington, DE: ISI Books, 2005), 464.

5. *Ghosts on the Roof: Selected Journalism of Whittaker Chambers* 1931–1959, ed., Terry Teachout (Washington, DC: Regnery Gateway, 1984), xiii.

6. Whittaker Chambers, *Witness* (Washington, DC: Regnery Publishing, 1980), 25–88. Chapter 1 entitled "Flight" provides an excellent narrative of Chambers's use of his Communist underground training to elude feared attacks against him in the aftermath of his break with the Communist underground.

7. *Ghosts on the Roof,* "Introduction," xiii.

8. *Ghosts on the Roof,* "Area of Decision," "Crisis," "Ghosts on the Roof," "Circles of Perdition," "The Tragic Sense of Life," and "Faith for a Lenten Age," 98–115, 150–65, and 184–93. These are, in particular, striking evidence not only of Chambers's literary prowess but of his willingness to engage the central events and thinkers of his time with his own notions of the good and the true.

9. *Ghosts on the Roof,* "Silence, Exile, and Death," 63–65.

10. Ibid., 65.

11. *Ghosts on the Roof,* "In Egypt Land," 134–40.

12. Ibid., 138.

13. Ibid., 140. The essay contains the following line: "Well might all Americans, at Christmas, 1946, ponder upon the fact that it is, like all the great problems of mankind, at bottom a religious problem. . . . It will, in fact, never be solved exclusively in human terms."

14. *Witness,* 25.

15. *Ghosts on the Roof,* "A Westminster Letter: To Temporize is Death," 308–12.

16. Ibid., 311.

17. *Witness,* 10. Chambers, in his foreword to *Witness,* entitled "Letter to my Children," articulated several themes that are foundational to his overall writing. One of the themes is the liberation from suffering and from traditional norms that man believes he has gained through the use of modern science and technology. Communism promised to bring such a notion to its most logical conclusion.

18. *Witness,* 11–12.

19. *Cold Friday,* "The Direct Glance," 87.

20. Ibid., 87.

21. Ibid., 86.

22. Ibid., 86.

23. Ibid., 88.

24. *Cold Friday,* ed., Duncan Norton Taylor (New York: Random House, 1964), 4–33, 152–53. The essays and correspondence in *Cold Friday* also develop Chambers's notion of the "counterrevolutionist," who, according to Chambers, cannot resist the temptation to give life, and, thus pursued by other means a politics that counters the Communist. The phrase "other means" is instructive because it connotes an unwillingness to inflict violence on the innocent. For conservatism to have any enduring value and a definite form it must now be understood as counterrevolution in Chambers's formulation.

25. *Cold Friday,* "Cold Friday," 38.

26. Ibid., 38.

27. Ibid., 48.

28. Aeschylus's *Prometheus Bound* in *The Complete Greek Tragedies,* ed., David Grene and Richmond Lattimore (Chicago: University of Chicago Press, 1959), 311.

29. *Cold Friday,* "Cold Friday" 41.Chambers states that he meant for his children to possess the soil as a sound reality they would always retain in some form.

30. Ibid., 41.

31. Ibid., 41.

32. *Odyssey of a Friend: Whittaker Chambers Letters to William F. Buckley, Jr., 1954–1961,* ed., William F. Buckley, Jr. (New York, NY: G. P. Putnam's Sons, 1969).

33. *Odyssey of a Friend,* 47–63.

34. Ibid., 205, 219–220.

35. Ibid., 48.

36. Ibid., 52.

37. Ibid., 57. Chambers was withering in his description of McCarthy: "He is a man fighting almost wholly by instinct and intuition, against forces for the most part coldly conscious of their ways, means, and ends. In other words, he scarcely knows what he is doing."

38. *Notes from the Underground: The Whittaker Chambers–Ralph de Toledano Letters 1949–1960,* ed., Ralph de Toledano (Washington, DC: Regnery Publishing, 1994).

39. *Notes from the Underground,* 23–25, 52–54.

40. Sam Tanenhaus, *Whittaker Chambers* (New York: Random House, Inc., 1998), 498. Tanenhaus notes that the play ended "mercifully."

41. *Notes from the Underground,* 196–240.

42. Ibid., 201.

43. Ibid., 204–5.

44. Ibid., 202.

45. Ibid., 204.

46. Ibid., 204.

47. *Witness*, 25.

48. Ibid., 25.

49. *Witness*, 25.

50. Ibid., 96; Wilbur Macey Stone, "Jay Chambers, Artist," *Bulletin of the New York Library*, vol. 34 (January 1930).

51. *Witness*, 93–95, 117.

52. Ibid., 117.

53. Several essays in *Cold Friday* evoke similar patterns of nature writing. In the essay "Cold Friday," Chambers describes the early spring life at Pipe Creek with his own dimming spirit:

> [W]e came upon a young blackthorn that had grown during seven years to a shrub higher than our heads, your mother wept—suddenly and briefly. That was the only deeper comment either of us made. As a younger man, I might have thought: "The world will pay for those tears," Now I know that the world has always been paying for them and always will. But we soon found where the bushes of the run were starred whitely by mats of bloodroot in flower. Elsewhere there were stretches of spring beauties. Along the Pipe Creek we found ourselves in beds of trout lilies in bloom. We had not known we had so many of them. As you know, trespassers sometimes vandalized our farther buildings and woods . . . We have no such worries with our wild flowers. No one else knows or cares that they are there. . . . Their beauty places them below the vision of one who cares little for beauty so they cadge their security from his blindness (61–62).

54. *Witness*, 140.

55. Ibid., 149, 173–75.

56. William Ernest Weld and Kathryn W. Sewny, *Herbert E. Hawkes,*

Dean of Columbia College, 1918–1943 (New York: Columbia University Press, 1958), 78.

57. Columbia application, Alger Hiss Papers, Harvard Law School Library (Cambridge, MA); In a note at the bottom of page 24 of WC, Tanenhaus noted that Mark van Doren, a literature professor of Chambers's and one of the leading intellectual lights on campus, had "rated Chambers the 'best' of all undergraduates he knew in the 1920s, surpassing Clifton Fadiman, John Gassner, Meyer Schapiro, the journalist Herbert Solow, Lionel Trilling, and Louis Zukofsky."

58. *Whittaker Chambers,* 25.

59. Ibid., 28.

60. *Witness,* 7. "It is in fact a total crisis—religious, moral, intellectual, social, political, economic."

61. *Cold Friday,* "Morningside," 135. Chambers highlighted the sights of another mass twentieth century phenomenon, refugees from military occupied regions. In this case, these were Rhinelanders fleeing from French troop occupation.

62. Ibid. Once awakened in the morning hours in Berlin, Chambers heard the following chant from a defiant Communist parade, "Grease the guillotine, grease the guillotine, grease the guillotine with the fat of tyrants. Blood must flow, blood must flow, blood, blood, blood."

63. *Cold Friday,* "Morningside," 114.

64. *Whittaker Chambers,* 30.

65. *Cold Friday,* "Morningside," 99.

66. Ibid., 99.

67. Ibid., 123.

68. Ibid., 92.

69. *Witness,* 89.

70. Ibid., 183.

71. "Personal History of Whittaker Chambers." FBI NY 65–14920, 151. "My brother's suicide set the seal on my being a Communist, I was a Communist before but I became a fanatical Communist afterwards."

72. *Witness,* 183.

73. *Whittaker Chambers,* 50.

74. Ralph de Toledano and Victor Lasky, *Seeds of Treason* (New York: Funk & Wagnalls, 1950), 14.

75. *Witness,* 215.

76. Ibid., 231–32. Chambers reported that Esther was a pacifist and not a Communist. Sent to report on striking textile workers she had became sympathetic to their situation and led the striking workers, according to Chambers, out of their police-enforced barricade.

77. *Whittaker Chambers,* 366–67.

78. *Witness,* 144–45.

79. Ibid., 368.

80. Ibid., 14–15.

81. Ibid.

82. Ibid., 15.

83. Ibid.

84. Ibid., 16.

85. Ibid., 9.

86. *Odyssey of a Friend,* 60.

87. Ibid., 61.

88. Ibid., 291.

Chapter 2: The Total Crisis

1. *Cold Friday,* "Morningside," 108–12.

2. Ibid., 109–10.

3. Ibid., 110–11.

4. Ibid., 111.

5. Ibid.

6. *Witness,* 25.

7. Karl Marx, *Early Writings,* ed. and trans. T.B. Bottomore (New York: McGraw-Hill Book Co., 1963), 206; Eric Voegelin, *Science, Politics & Gnosticism* (Wilmington, DE: ISI Books, 2004), 17–20. In the same-titled

essay Voegelin argues the following point: "This being, which is itself nature, also stands over against nature and assists it in its development by human labor—which in its highest form is technology and industry based on the natural sciences." Voegelin concludes from this analysis, "The purpose of this speculation is to shut off the process of being from transcendent being and have man create himself" (18).

8. *Witness,* 9.

9. *Cold Friday,* "The Direct Glance," 69.

10. *Ghosts on the Roof,* "The Devil," 173–74. In "The Devil," which features a dialogue between a nightclub patron and Satan, Satan explains the following thought on man's suffering and creativity: "For at the heart of all human suffering is the anguish of the chance that that creative seed of goodness, that little flash of inward light, however brief, may not perpetuate itself, that a man can leave this life this light, without communicating that one cell of himself which is real."

11. *Ghosts on the Roof,* "Faith for a Lenten Age," 189–90.

12. *Cold Friday,* "The Direct Glance," 69–70.

13. *Ghosts on the Roof,* "Faith for a Lenten Age." Although Chambers is explaining Niebuhr's Christian anthropology, his positive evaluation of Niebuhr's views on man coincides well with the analysis of man's condition in "Letter to my Children." The general tenor of this essay strongly indicates that Chambers identified with Niebuhr's views.

14. *Odyssey of a Friend,* 121.

15. *Cold Friday,* "The Direct Glance," 69.

16. Ibid., 69–70.

17. Ibid., 70.

18. Ibid.

19. Ibid.

20. Ibid.

21. *Ghosts on the Roof,* "A Westminster Letter: To Temporize is Death," 308–12. In this essay, "A Westminster Letter: To Temporize is Death" Chambers recounted the Hungarian resistance and the opportunities for

advance against Communism that it opened for the West and which, in turn, the West squandered.

22. *Ghosts on the Roof*, "Crisis," 104–10. In the essay "Crisis," published in 1944, Chambers not only skewered the Roosevelt Administration for its lack of political prudence in recalling General Joseph Stilwell, the organizer of American efforts on behalf Chinese Nationalist forces, but also implicated the Administration for failing to understand the unity of Communist efforts internationally and the enormous problems created for America by a Communist China.

23. *Ghosts on the Roof,* "A Westminster Letter: To Temporize is Death," 308–12.

24. John Lewis Gaddis, *The Cold War: A New History* (New York: Penguin Group Inc., 2005). Gaddis argues that subsequent access to reams of Soviet archival material has tended to confirm, although not citing Chambers specifically, observations made by Chambers and others regarding the ideological motivations in the reasoning process of Soviet leaders, particularly in projections of force.

25. *Cold Friday,* "The Direct Glance," 72.

26. Ibid., 71.

27. Ibid.

28. Ibid., 72.

29. Ibid., 73.

30. Ibid.

31. Ibid.

32. *Witness*, 16. Chambers makes the argument that liberty in the West is a political reading of the Bible. A constant in Chambers's thought is the divine guarantee that must underlie and direct human action.

33. Ibid., 73.

34. Ibid., 74.

35. Ibid., 74.

36. Ibid., 85–86.

37. Ibid., 86.

38. Ibid.

39. Ibid., 86–87.

40. *Odyssey of a Friend,* 154.

41. *Cold Friday,* "Pipe Creek Farm," 12–16. "But a civilization which supposes that what it chiefly has to offer mankind is more abundant bread—that civilization is already half-dead. Sooner or later it will know it as it chokes on a satiety of that bread by which alone men cannot live. It will, in all probability, know it long before. For it seems to be a law of life and of history that societies in which the pursuit of abundance and comfort has displaced all other pursuits in importance cease to be societies" (*Cold Friday,* 14–15).

42. *Odyssey of a Friend,* 154.

43. Ibid., 154.

44. William F. Buckley, Jr., *National Review,* July 6, 1979, 879. This is a column offered by Buckley after the elevation of Karol Józef Wojtyla to the See of Peter. The import of Buckley's argument is that Cardinal Wyszynski, the leader of Polish Catholics under both Nazi and Soviet rule, had invigorated and preserved the witness of the Church in Poland. The fruits of his episcopal statesmanship were now seen in a Polish pope and an animated Polish Catholicism operating behind the Iron Curtain. The interesting connection Buckley made in the piece was to Chambers's acute moral sense that the spirit of an authentic resistance had broken through in Poland decades ago.

45. *Odyssey of a Friend,* 159–60.

46. Ibid., 159–60.

47. Ibid., 160.

48. *Witness,* 4.

49. Ibid., 459–63.

50. Ibid., 461.

51. Ibid., 458.

52. Ibid., 462–63.

53. *Whittaker Chambers,* 160. Isaac Don Levine, a journalist for the

Saturday Evening Post, in an apparent bid to secure Chambers's aid as an informant reported to him that Krivitsky was certain the intelligence Chambers handled as an underground agent would end up in Berlin aiding the Nazi war effort.

54. *Whittaker Chambers,* 161–63. Berle's testimony at the Hiss trial in certain respects ignored or misrepresented the facts of this visit between Chambers and Berle. Berle's notes from his interview of Chambers demonstrated the inadequacy of his testimony, which underplayed the extent of Communist membership and espionage within the State Department and other departments of the federal government. The notes also serve as direct evidence that the federal government had knowledge of Hiss, among others, and did relatively little.

55. *Whittaker Chambers,* 161–63. Many of the names Chambers disclosed to Berle were new to him: Laurence Duggan, Alger Hiss, Donald Hiss, Noel Field and Lauchlin Currie, a special assistant to FDR. Duggan and the Hiss brothers currently held positions in the State Department. Field had moved on from the State Department to a post at the League of Nations. Accounts differ on what precisely Berle did with the evidence. The consensus position is that Berle never pursued the accusations with any great vigor, surprisingly, given the circumstances, international and domestic, surrounding the accusations.

56. *Ghosts on the Roof,* "The Ghosts on the Roof," 111. The piece received great criticism after its publication in 1945 given the consensus position that Soviet–American collaboration was possible and necessary to European peace.

57. Ibid., 112.

58. Ibid.

59. Ibid., 114.

60. Ibid.

61. Ibid.

62. *Ghosts on the Roof,* "Introduction," xxiii. When reprinted in 1948 the preemptive, sympathetic tag affixed to the piece in 1945 supporting

Soviet–U.S. collaboration was replaced with a simple note that recommended the short story to all interested observers. Chambers's view had now become almost prophetic.

63. The substantial earthquake in economics produced by the writings of British economist John Maynard Keynes also loomed large in this shift to the necessity of central coordination of markets. The response by Austrian economist Friedrich Hayek, in his essay, "The Use of Information in a Free Society," published in 1948 by the *American Economic Review*, argued that the very nature of calculating information in a diverse modern economy made central coordination a logical impossibility. Gathering and utilizing information in an efficient manner required that private persons and business entities be the primary economic actors. This was primarily because government committees, councils, and boards of experts were unable to both gather and profitably use real-time data integral to production, manufacture, supply, and selling of goods and services.

64. *Ghosts on the Roof,* "The Revolt of the Intellectuals," 60.

65. Ibid.

66. *Witness,* 4.

67. *Ghosts on the Roof,* Section 4: The History of Western Culture, 197–253.

68. *Ghosts on the Roof,* "The Middle Ages," 201.

Chapter 3: *Tragedy and Hope*

1. *Cold Friday,* "Pipe Creek Farm," 11.

2. Ibid.

3. *Witness,* 4–5.

4. Ibid., 5.

5. Ibid.

6. *Katyn: A Crime Without Punishment,* ed., Anne M. Cienciala, Natalia S. Lebedeva, and Wojciech Materski (New Haven, CT: Yale University Press, 2008).

7. *Cold Friday,* "Pipe Creek Farm," 20.

8. Ibid., 20

9. Ibid.

10. *Odyssey of a Friend,* 186–87.

11. Ibid., 187.

12. Ibid.

13. Ibid.

14. Ibid.

15. Ibid.

16. *Witness,* 78. On the purges of the original revolutionaries of 1917, Chambers stated, "The charge, on which they were one and all destroyed, the charge that they had betrayed their handiwork, was incredible. They were the Communist Party. If the charge was true, then every other Communist had given his life for a fraud. If the charge was false, then every other Communist was giving his life for a fraud. This was a torturing thought. No Communist could escape it."

17. *Witness,* 79.

18. Ibid., 81.

19. *Odyssey of a Friend,* 265.

20. *Witness,* 81.

21. Ibid., 81.

22. *Cold Friday,* "Pipe Creek Farm," 19.

23. *Witness,* 82–83.

24. Ibid., 83. Chambers stated, "What I had been fell from me like dirty rags. The rags that fell from me were not only Communism. What fell was the whole web of the materialist modern mind—the luminous shroud which it has spun about the spirit of man, paralyzing in the name of rationalism the instinct of his soul for God, denying in the name of knowledge the reality of the soul and its birthright in that mystery on which mere knowledge falters and shatters at every step."

25. *Whittaker Chambers,* 71. On the voice Chambers found in the series of short stories he penned for *The New Masses,* Tanenhaus notes that

"Chambers seeks to ennoble the idiom, roughhewn yet also poetic, of simple heroes risen from the soil." Tanenhuas also cites luminaries of the "literary left" like Alpert Halper and Granville Hicks who "still rated Chambers's story ("Can You Make Out Their Voices") among the best to come out of the Communist movement." Granville Hicks, *A Part of the Truth* (New York, NY: Harcourt, 1965), 95. Alpert Halper, *Good-bye, Union Square: A Writer's Memoir of the Thirties* (Chicago: Quadrangle, 1970), 113.

26. *Ghosts on the Roof,* Section One: A Member of the Revolution, 3–46.

27. *Witness,* 262–63.

28. Ibid.

29. *Ghosts on the Roof,* "You Have Seen the Heads," 22–29.

30. Ibid., 29.

31. *Witness,* 263. On the short stories published by the New Masses Chambers remarks, "it is easy to see that the stories are scarcely about Communism at all. Communism is the context in which they are told . . . In each, it is not the political situation, but the spirit of man which is triumphant."

32. *Ghosts on the Roof,* "The Devil," 166–74.

33. Ibid., 167.

34. Ibid., 173.

35. *Ghosts on the Roof,* "Faith for a Lenten Age," 184–96. This essay also involves discussion of the Swiss Reformed theologian Karl Barth and Danish philosopher Sören Kierkegaard's understanding of the tragic sense of man. One detects that Barth's conversion from progressivism resulting from World War I and his consequent reconsideration of biblical texts were compelling inducements to Chambers's favorable reception of him.

36. *Ghosts on the Roof,* "Faith for a Lenten Age," 189–90.

37. Ibid., 189.

38. Ibid.

39. Ibid., 190.

40. Ibid. Chambers quoted Niebuhr to the effect that "to purge even moral achievement of sin is not so easy as moralists imagine."

41. Ibid., 191. Rendering the situation tolerable for Chambers are the theological virtues that lead man through his own deficits of existence.

42. Ibid.

43. Ibid.

44. *Ghosts on the Roof,* "The Middle Ages" and "The Protestant Revolution," 197–208, 242–56. This look back to a premodern Christianity and early Reformationist theology was prefigured by Chambers in a series of essays he wrote for Time along with Jacques Barzun, among other luminaries. Designed to be a survey of Western civilization, Chambers's essays "The Middle Ages," "Medieval Life," and "The Protestant Reformation" are written in a tone of high admiration for a civilization that still looked above itself to God for direction, guidance, and purpose while displaying such understandings, however dimly perceived, in its culture and the force of its commitments.

45. *Witness,* 193. Chambers related that as a student he wondered, "Can a man go on living in a world that is dying? If he can, what should he do in the crisis of the twentieth century?"

46. Ibid., 196.

47. Ibid., 11.

48. Ibid., 194.

49. Ibid., 194–95.

50. Ibid., 444.

51. Ibid.

52. Ibid.

53. Ibid.

54. Eric J. Sundquist's "*Witness* Recalled," *Commentary,* Volume 86, Number 6 (December 1988), 57–63. This essay provides an excellent analysis of the many literary allusions made by Chambers in *Witness.*

55. *Witness,* 70–74. "But, with this hope at the bottom of my mind, I thought that simply by seeing Alger again, by talking quietly with him,

I might pry him lose from the party. In any case, I could never have acted with him as I had with [Harry Dexter] White and the others; our friendship made it unthinkable" (*Witness,* 70).

56. Ibid., 72. Chambers reported that Priscilla Hiss's exact response to his confession of having left the party because of the fundamental corruption of Communism was the following: "What you have been saying is just mental masturbation."

57. "*Witness* Recalled," 62.

58. Ibid., 450.

59. Ibid.

60. Ibid.

61. *Odyssey of a Friend,* 133. In a similar vein, Chambers recounted in *Witness,* "Since the Purge, millions of men, women, and children in the world have died violently. The 20th century has put out of its mind, because it can no longer cope with the enormity of the statistic, the millions it has exterminated in its first fifty years," (78).

62. Ibid., 133.

Chapter 4: The Conservative Spirit

1. *Odyssey of a Friend,* 185.

2. Ibid., 97–98; see also, *Notes from the Underground,* 23. Here, Chambers states that he is a conservative as a logical consequence of more substantial philosophical-theological commitments. This remark, pulled from correspondence written in 1950 regarding Diana Trilling's criticism of Chambers's alleged inveterate Manichean tendencies, is more likely not dispositive of Chambers's political position. Chambers's overall theme in the letter and in his approach to liberal anti-Communists was that their program was inadequate in the ongoing fight with Communism.

3. *Witness,* 17. Chambers notes in other writings the centrality of property and the market to any decent regime.

4. *Odyssey of a Friend,* 137–38.

5. Ibid., 138.

6. Ibid., 137.

7. *Notes from the Underground*, 162–63.

8. Ibid.

9. *Ghosts on the Roof,* "The Middle Ages," 197–208 and "The Protestant Revolution," 242–64; Eric Voegelin, *Hitler and the Germans,* ed., Detlev Clemens and Brendan Purcell (Columbia, MO: University of Missouri Press, 1999), 118. Eric Voegelin's interpretation argues that the modern ideologue is a type of reincarnation of the ancient "gnostics." These gnostics found their salvation in a secretive knowledge liberating them from the burden of reality. The modern ideologue replicated this intellectual falsity with his denial of the structure of reality—the ground of man's being—in favor of an abstracted ideology. In turn, the violence inherent in modern dissolutions was unleashed. The paradox is that the denial of the structure of reality is never complete; one always is thrown back into the very reality that one denies. Thus, an intense anger at the inherent limitedness of human existence and the inability to stay in one's preferred ideological reality issues into the constant acts of avoidance, despair, and death-dealing by the gnostic. Eric Voegelin's *The New Science of Politics: An Introduction* (Chicago: University of Chicago Press, 1987), 162–89.

10. *Ghosts on the Roof,* 260.

11. Ibid., 263.

12. Ibid.

13. Ibid., "The Middle Ages," 197–203.

14. Ibid., 242–53.

15. Ibid., 243.

16. *Cold Friday,* "A Man of the Right," 226.

17. *Odyssey of a Friend,* 75–78. Chambers, of course, never endorsed the argument of moral equivalency. The murders and nihilistic acts committed by the Narodniki were not justified by the oppression of Tsarist governments. The difference is substantial between the martyr and his witness to a greater truth, and those who kill not only themselves but others in acts of homicidal violence.

18. Ibid., 77. "For the spirit of the Narodniki, all that was soldierly and saintly in the revolution, found its last haven, O irony!, in the Fourth Section (one purpose of the Great Purge was to kill it out once for all). The appeal to the Narodniki was offered by Chambers to explain his apparent differences with Willi Schlamm, a founding editor of *National Review.* Schlamm, like Chambers a former man of the Left, had never entered into the spiritual bond with Communism that Chambers had formed with the ideology. Thus, Schlamm remained unable to understand the particular tack Chambers wanted to take against the Left, in particular, with the new publication. Here, Chambers argued that his prior revolutionary status afforded him peculiar and bizarre insights into the modern Left, necessary to the success of any counterrevolutionary movement.

19. *Witness,* 6; *Odyssey of a Friend,* 77. "And I have told what that meant to me at one moment; how, had my comrade Sazonov, not done that, there would not have been a Hiss Case as we know it. This spirit persisted in the Fourth Section as late as 1938."

20. *Cold Friday,* "A Man of the Right," 229.

21. Ibid., 221.

22. Ibid. Chambers, however, had been crucial to ensuring that *The Conservative Mind* received an initial favorable review in the *Saturday Evening Post.* This event was seen by many observers as crucial to the book's early success.

23. Ibid.

24. Ibid., 222

25. Ibid.

26. Ibid.

27. *Odyssey of a Friend,* 242.

28. Ibid.

29. Ibid., 85.

30. Ibid., 98.

31. *Whittaker Chambers,* 235. Nixon's strategy in the hearings was never to prove outright that Hiss was a Communist, but to show that Hiss

knew Chambers, which would establish that Hiss was dishonest given his frank denial of ever having known Chambers.

32. Ibid., 231. Tanenhaus argues that Nixon received information on Hiss's suspected Communist sympathies from several sources, namely, a Catholic priest, Rev. John Cronin, and J. Edgar Hoover's FBI, which leaked files to Nixon on a regular basis. Earl Mazo, *Richard Nixon: A Political and Personal Portrait* (New York: Harper, 1959), 51. Reverend John Cronin, SS, "The Problem of American Communism in 1945: Facts and Recommendations: A Confidential Study for Private Circulation," 37, 49; Allen Weinstein, "Nixon vs. Hiss," *Esquire* (November 1975), 76.

33. *Odyssey of a Friend,* 104–7.

34. William F. Buckley, Jr., *National Review,* "The Prophet," 879, July 6, 1979. "I have been a Wyszynski man *ab initio.* I have argued that no other course was possible. I am afraid that I have deeply disappointed (perhaps even estranged) certain Catholic friends by my unbudgeability on this point. I point [to] . . . the contrasting attitudes of their Cardinals. No one who has not suffered so much may judge Cardinal Mindszenty, even if he were stupid enough to incline to. But contrasting policy results can be appreciated; I hold that the contrast favors the results in Poland."

35. Ibid. Chambers's analysis might also contribute to a misreading of the situation in Hungary and Poland. Important Cold War commentators have noted that Mindszenty faced a far more aggressive and violent regime than the one faced by Wyszynski in Poland. Wyszynski had more space to root the church and gain a degree of insulation from Soviet pressure than did Mindszenty. The Hungarian Cardinal may have had little choice in accepting imprisonment and exile. Thus Mindszenty, as Chambers noted elsewhere on the balancing acts of conservatives, was one who could compromise no longer and still preserve his integrity of conscience.

36. As Buckley commented on this letter from Chambers, "who can deny that those of us who thought Mindszenty right, Wyszynski wrong, lacked the prophetic insight of Chambers." Ibid.

37. *Cold Friday,* 235.

38. Ibid., 226–32.

39. Ibid., 227, 236–37.

40. Ibid., 227, 232–38.

41. Ibid., 232.

42. Ibid.

43. Ibid.

44. *Odyssey of a Friend,* 142–43.

45. Ibid.

46. Ibid., 219.

47. Ibid., 220.

48. Ibid., 216.

49. Ibid., 229.

50. *Cold Friday,* "A Man of the Right," 232–36; *Ghosts on the Roof,* "A Westminster Letter: From Springhead to Springhead," 319–25.

51. *Cold Friday,* 233.

52. *Ghosts on the Roof,* 323.

53. *Odyssey of a Friend,* 228. "But I claim that capitalism is not, and by its essential nature cannot conceivably be, conservative."

54. Ibid. Chambers records in *Cold Friday* that the Civil War was the assertion of control by an industrial modern order of the Northern states over the opposing agrarian section of the Southern states (*Cold Friday,* 39).

55. Ibid., 129–30. Alexis de Tocqueville made a similar observation: "So, of all the countries in the world, America is the one in which the precepts of Descartes are least studied and best followed. No one should be surprised at that." Alexis de Tocqueville's *Democracy in America,* Volume II (New York: Harper & Row Publishers, 1966), 429.

56. Ibid., 229.

57. *Cold Friday,* 235.

58. Ibid., 228.

59. *Ghosts on the Roof,* "Big Sister is Watching You," 315.

60. Ibid., 312–15. Chambers, the literary aesthete, found aesthetic reasons to dislike Rand's novel in its poor artistic capability and style. A novel whose central feature is a forty-page monologue on the libertarian application of Aristotelian ethics was certainly not of a high literary order in Chambers's mind.

61. Ibid., 317.

62. Ibid.

63. Ibid., 318.

64. *Odyssey of a Friend*, 141–42; *Notes from the Underground*, 279–81.

65. *Odyssey of a Friend*, 142.

66. *Notes from the Underground*, 280.

Chapter 5: The Ascent from Modernity

1. I am mindful that the Enlightenment was not a univocal expression of philosophical modernity and consisted of several varied elements, some better than others. However, while Chambers does not state precisely which Enlightenment project he found odious to true thought, his commentary primarily speaks to the Continental Enlightenment as typified by René Descartes, Baruch Spinoza, and Immanuel Kant. Moreover, Chambers drank deeply from Henri de Lubac's *The Drama of Atheist Humanism* which explicates the hyperrationalist visions of Ludwig Feuerbach, Auguste Comte, Karl Marx, and Friedrich Nietzsche.

2. *Odyssey of a Friend*, 187. "It is not whim that has brought certain Catholics to seek to reconcile Thomism and Existentialism. It is reality and the age. It is not the truths, but the little power of man, caught between them and a reality which crushes him, that is in question; so that, in our time, it is given each of us to understand what was said from the Cross: "My God, my God, why hast Thou abandoned me?"

3. Irving Howe, "God, Man, and Stalin," *Nation*, May 24, 1952, reprinted in *Alger Hiss, Whittaker Chambers, and the Schism in the American Soul*, ed., Patrick A. Swan (Wilmington, DE: ISI Books, 2004): 81–90. Howe's piece represents in modular form the view that the real vil-

lain in the Hiss case was Chambers. Not only wrong on the facts, in making the allegations Chambers unduly threatened the civil liberties and social order of the country by igniting the threat of the intolerant masses against anyone who was a liberal in American political life. For a more contemporary example of this same reasoning see John Lukacs's "Whittaker Chambers" in *Remembered Past* (Wilmington, DE: ISI Books, 2005), 349–52.

4. *Witness*, 471.

5. Ibid., 33.

6. Ibid., 471.

7. Leslie Fiedler, "Hiss, Chambers, and the Age of Innocence," *Commentary*, August 1951, reprinted in *Alger Hiss, Whittaker Chambers, and the Schism of the American Soul*, 1–26. Fiedler reports that Berle reported Chambers accusations to an incredulous Acheson who investigated by asking Donald Hiss, Alger's brother, if he was a Communist. Donald said no, and Acheson was "satisfied" and did not pursue the matter further (23).

8. *Witness*, 472.

9. Ibid., 472–73.

10. Diana Trilling, "A Memorandum on the Hiss Case," *Partisan Review*, May–June 1950, reprinted in *Alger Hiss, Whittaker Chambers, and the Schism of the American Soul*, 27–48.

11. Ibid., 40–48.

12. Unlike Chambers, many of these idealists of the Left, while shocked by the Nazi–Soviet Pact of 1938, were not led to fundamentally re-engage their most deep-seated assumptions and principles by the fact of two totalitarian powers joining forces, entailing, as the Pact did, the virtual dismissal of the Popular Front by the Soviet Union.

13. Diana Trilling, "A Memorandum on the Hiss Case," *Partisan Review*, May–June 1950, reprinted in *Alger Hiss, Whittaker Chambers, and the Schism of the American Soul*, 34–35; Francois Furet's *The Passing of an Illusion*, trans. Deborah Furet (Chicago: University of Chicago Press,

1999). The French theorist François Furet advanced a similar thesis in this highly-regarded treatment of the totalitarian allure.

14. *Schism,* 40.

15. Leslie Fiedler, "Hiss, Chambers, and the Age of Innocence," *Commentary,* August 1951, reprinted in *Alger Hiss, Whittaker Chambers, and the Schism of the American Soul,* 1–26.

16. Ibid., 25.

17. Diana Trilling, "A Memorandum on the Hiss Case," *Partisan Review,* May–June 1950, reprinted in *Alger Hiss, Whittaker Chambers, and the Schism of the American Soul,* 43.

18. *Witness,* 473.

19. Ibid., 474.

20. Arthur Schlesinger, Jr., "Whittaker Chambers & His 'Witness,'" *Saturday Review,* May 24, 1952.

21. *Witness,* 787.

22. Ibid., 25.

23. Ibid., 84. In making what Chambers described as "the impossible return," he reported the following experience: "One day as I came down the stairs in Mount Royal Terrace house, the question of the impossible return struck me with sudden sharpness. I thought: 'You cannot do it. No one can go back.' As I stepped down into the dark hall, I found myself stopped, not by a constraint, but by a hush of my whole being. In this organic hush, a voice said with perfect distinctness: 'If you will fight for freedom, all will be well with you.'"

24. *Ghosts on the Roof,* "Faith for a Lenten Age," 184–93, 188. Adding to Chambers's understanding of God is his essay on Franz Kafka, "The Tragic Sense of Life," where he argues that Kafka's writing urges its reader to consider the vast separation of man and God and the grace that inexplicably falls on certain men. The implication is that man should consider his own ideas and existence as inherently limited and conditioned by the divine.

25. "Faith for a Lenten Age," 188.

26. Chambers listed *The Possessed* as one of the most important novels he read, which vitally shaped his understanding of modern ideology and the terms it sought to impose and the creative imagination needed to combat it.

27. Sam Tanenhaus, "Whittaker Chambers, Man of Letters," *New Criterion,* April 1990, reprinted in *Alger Hiss, Whittaker Chambers, and the Schism of the American Soul,* 278.

28. *Witness,* 4.

29. Ibid., 9.

30. Ibid.

31. Ibid., 16.

32. Ibid.

33. Ibid., 16–17.

34. Ibid.

35. John Sullivan, *The President, the Pope, and the Prime Minister: Three Who Changed the World* (Washington, DC: Regnery Publishing Inc., 2006).

36. I recall, here, Ronald Reagan who stated loudly that his views on Communism and the Soviet Union had been largely shaped by Chambers's autobiography. In addition to statesmen like Reagan and Thatcher, or the leadership of Charles de Gaulle during the 1968 Parisian riots, certain leaders and articulators of refined and conservative sensibilities in the United States, Britain, and Western Europe provided invaluable resources to the replenishment of a more heroic and robust understanding of human liberty throughout the Cold War than that offered by social democratic liberals.

Acknowledgments

The IDEA FOR THIS BOOK emerged from research I conducted for a graduate students' conference that explored totalitarianism as an inherent aspect of philosophical modernity. To that end, several thinkers aided me greatly in my initial research and throughout the writing of the book. However, overwhelming gratitude is owed to my wife, Evelyn, who permitted me the ample time for the work that went into this project. At several moments, when I believed that I was no match for uncovering Whittaker Chambers, it was my wife who listened to and guided my writing towards a more even and skillful appreciation of his life and ideas. Absent her affection, this project would have broken upon the first shoals it encountered. The unbought grace of my wife's love and her unmatched devotion to Augustine, Clare, and Noah Benedict, constantly reminds me of how incomplete a life is without the love that sanctifies this temporal existence.

Dan Mahoney, who has always insisted on the thoughtful understanding of those significant thinkers who maintained a critical distance from modern liberalism, substantially deepened the book's analysis in many important ways. His prior writings on Chambers and Aleksandr Solzhenitsyn inspired much of the spirit of this project. Indeed, Mahoney's insistence on the recovery of premodern wisdom, as displayed by thinkers like Chambers and Solzhenitsyn, and its necessary blending with certain habits of modernity is, quite simply, conservatism at its best.

James Bruce was most helpful throughout the life of this project. For sharing his exceptional and envied talents with me, I am most grateful. In eagerness do many of us wait for Bruce's own forthcoming contributions that will aid our dim understandings of the current order we inhabit.

The dean of historians of American conservatism, George Nash, read the early manuscript and shared several ideas for ordering the overall work that were highly ameliorative. For sharing his time, learning, and wisdom to me during this project, I am very grateful.

I must also thank Brad Birzer and Lee Cheek for their comments and advice on certain chapters of this book. The patience and guidance that Brad displayed towards early manifestations of the project were encouraging in many ways.

A final word of thanks is owed to my editors Jed Donahue and Christian Tappe. In addition to their high professionalism and understanding of the depth of Chambers's project, Jed and Christian's editorial abilities greatly aided the clear expression of the ideas contained in this book.

Index